Great Passenger Ships of the World

Volume 1: 1858–1912

Kaiser Wilhelm der Grosse

Great Passenger Ships of the World

Volume 1: 1858–1912

Arnold Kludas

Translated by Charles Hodges

Patrick Stephens, Wellingborough

First published in Germany under the
title *Die Grossen Passagierschiffe der Welt.*
First published in Great Britain
October 1975

10   9   8   7   6   5

ISBN 0-85059-174-0

*Patrick Stephens Limited is part of the
Thorsons Publishing Group*

Printed in Great Britain by
Butler & Tanner Ltd, Frome and London

Introduction

In view of the appearance during recent years of a large number of books on passenger shipping, the question as to the necessity for a further work on this subject is understandable and justified. Among the many published are books about individual companies, about particular services, about ships contemporary to particular periods of time, as well as others produced against selected criteria. They are all the result of excellent research. However there has not up to now been an illustrated collective documentation, and this work is intended to close the gap in respect of the great passenger liners. On the appearance of the fifth volume there will be presented for the first time in international shipping literature a work covering all passenger ships to date of over 10,000 GRT, with all essential technical and historical data with, furthermore, the appearance of the ships recorded in photographs.

I would answer as follows the inevitable question as to why the gross registered tonnage limit has been set at 10,000:

1 Any other figure would have provoked the same question.

2 A compilation in the present form and detail to cover all the world's passenger ships built to date would, in the light of the results of current maritime research, be beyond the capacity of one single author. Such a work might perhaps be possible from an international team of authors, but:

3 the cost of such a project would probably deter any publisher from implementing it.

All technical and historical information in this work is supported by careful comparison with listed material, it having been nearly always possible to set right conflicting information by reference to primary sources. Remaining contradictions are noted in the text. I shall always be grateful for further information and corrections — with sources, please.

This volume deals with the period 1858–1912. As an anachronistic forerunner, the Great Eastern of 1858 was the first passenger ship of over 10,000 GRT to be placed in service. With the launching 30 years later of the 10,000-tonner City of New York this limit was again exceeded, but with the results of subsequent technical development to her advantage. In the following years the steady expansion of world traffic brought about bigger and bigger ships on all routes. With the Olympic and Titanic, 1911/12 saw placed in service the first passenger ships of over 40,000 GRT.

I should like to record my very sincere thanks to all those who have helped me in the preparation of this work, and personally for their willing and energetic support the following: Dr Herbert Bischoff, Reinfeld; Mr N. R. P. Bonsor, Jersey; Mr Frank O. Braynard, Sea Cliff; Mr Laurence Dunn, Gravesend; Herr Hans Graf, Hamburg; Mr Stephen Kentwell, Tokyo; Dr E. H. Kuhlman, Munich; Herr Hans Jürgen Mayburg, Bremen; M J. F. van Puyvelde, Brussels; M Paul E. R. Scarceriaux, Brussels; and Mr Paul H. Silverstone, New York. I also owe special thanks to my wife, Ursula, who with great understanding has always supported me in my work.

Arnold Kludas

Hamburg: March, 1975.

Foreword

Probably at no time in the last 50 years has interest in passenger ships been so great as it is today. This is perhaps understandable, for when something is with us we tend to take it for granted. Again, particularly with this type of ship, interest at any one time has tended to be focused either on the very new or, in certain instances, on those elderly liners which somehow established themselves as timeless favourites – all this at the expense of those mid-way through their careers.

As my good friend Arnold Kludas so rightly stresses, this book and the rest of the series together provide something which is unique: completeness of coverage within the well chosen limits of size and period. Many readers will doubtless have been familiar with certain vessels of a particular decade or range of services, say on the Atlantic, but not so with those used on other trades. Here all are presented with the same meticulous care and precision by someone who can be trusted to avoid the pitfalls which have trapped so many. In this unbiased approach we see the touch of the true historian. With such a large field to cover many authors would have been content merely to portray the ships as they had been in their prime, but a notable feature of this series is the large number of rare and often unique illustrations depicting these, the world's passenger liners, in the later stages of their careers.

Laurence Dunn
(Member, Belgian Nautical Research Association; Vice-President, World Ship Society)

Timbers, 18 Lennox Road, Gravesend, Kent.

Explanatory Notes

All passenger ships ever launched having a gross registered tonnage (GRT) of over 10,000 are presented in the five volumes of this work. Volume I herewith deals with the period from 1858 to 1912.

The ships are arranged chronologically, with the exception of sister-ships or groups of ships which have been placed together regardless of exact chronology. The chronological order of the individual sections has been determined from the launching date of the first ship of the class or group. The technical/historical biography of each ship appears under the name with which the ship first entered service. This applies also if the ship sailed later under other names and for other shipping companies. This rule is departed from only in exceptional circumstances. To trace a particular ship the reader is recommended to use the Index of Ships' Names, pages 214/216. In cases where ships have been renamed I have included after the first name in each case, as a further help in tracing, all the later names, each with the year of the name-change.

The following is a guide to the technical and historical information concerning the ships.

I. Technical Data

The information given in the paragraph on technical data applies fundamentally for the date when the ship first went into service as a passenger carrier. In the case of incompleted ships for which at their respective stages of construction this had not been finally decided upon, I have given the planned specifications. Alterations affecting technical data are noted with historical data against the appropriate dates.

Dimensions Length overall × moulded breadth in metres rounded off to one place of decimals, followed by the equivalent in feet, the length to the nearest whole number and breadth to one place of decimals. Length overall has been adopted in preference to other length measurements. It was found that recorded registered length and length between perpendiculars could vary from time to time and from place to place.

Propulsion Type of machinery, constructor. Where the shipbuilder has not been responsible for the propelling machinery, its constructor is given. The abbreviations III or IV exp eng indicate triple or quadruple expansion (steam) engines.

Power The figure of horse power given is the highest performance attainable by the engines in normal service. The different methods of measuring horse power, according to the form of propulsion, are as follows:
IHP = indicated horse power, unit of measurement for reciprocating steam engines and internal combustion engines.
SHP = shaft horse power, for turbine machinery and internal combustion engines.
BHP = brake horse power, unit for measurement for internal combustion engines.

Speed Service speed is given in knots. This is followed, as far as can be established, by the highest speed achieved on trials with the engines running at maximum power.

Passengers On nearly all ships the passenger accommodation and the number of berths for each class were frequently altered. Even if it were still possible to-day to establish all these changes exactly, the necessary effort would not justify the value of the figures thus obtained. One can come to completely different conclusions however correct the figures, for sofa-berths or emergency beds may or may not have been included. The information on alterations to passenger accommodation therefore is limited to really significant modifications, as far as it has been possible to determine them. In the case of the older ships which are dealt with in this volume, it is often impossible to differentiate clearly between third class and steerage. The standard in the lowest-priced classes of passenger accommodation varied from ship to ship, and between owners and routes, from large primitive mass dormitories (which could be used alternatively for the carriage of cargo) to relatively comfortably equipped rooms with a moderate number of beds. On many ships these variations existed side by side under the general description of 'third class'. One can reasonably assume that on a three-class ship with a large third class capacity, a considerable number of the latter passengers would be accommodated in dormitories. The description 'steerage' is therefore appropriate.

Crew Crew-strength also was subject to alteration, as for instance when a ship was converted from coal to oil-firing, or when the passenger capacity was changed. Changes in crew-strength have not been noted. Unfortunately it has not been possible to determine this figure for every ship.

II. Historical Data

The historical information reflects in chronological order the career of the ship, giving all important events and facts.

Owners In the ships' biographies, shipowners are indicated throughout by what are considered to be the accepted short-forms in English-speaking countries. Nevertheless, a selected short-form may not itself be based on an English translation of a non-English title, for instance: Nippon Yusen KK, CGT, etc. It is assumed that Cie, Cia, AG, SA, etc, will be as familiar to readers as are such English abbreviations as

Contents

SN, SS, Co, Corp, etc. After the name of a shipowner, the location mentioned in each case is the ship's home port, which is not necessarily where the shipowner has his head office.

An alphabetical list of all shipowners with their complete styles is included as an appendix to Volume V.

It should be pointed out that the following shipping companies were from 1902 combined in the International Mercantile Marine Company of the American banker, John Pierpoint Morgan: the American Line, the Atlantic Transport Line, the Dominion Line, the Leyland Line, the Red Star Line and the White Star Line.

These companies continued to operate independently but their capital belonged to J.P. Morgan. The foregoing explains the remarkably large number of transfers and sales within this group of companies.

Builders Like shipowners, builders are noted throughout by their accepted short-forms, and are listed alphabetically with their complete styles in Volume V.

Completion Completion-date is the date of commencement of trials.

Routes Ports of call are omitted from the information concerning routes.

The Great Eastern

Steamship *Great Eastern*
Great Ship Co, London
Launched as *Leviathan*

Builders: J. Scott Russell & Co, Millwall, London
18,915 GRT; 210.0 × 25.3 m / 689 × 82.8 ft; Two oscillating steam engines: one engine for the paddles, from hull-builders, 3,400 IHP; one engine for the single screw from Watt & Co, London, 4,900 IHP; Sail area: 5,100 sq m / 54,900 sq ft; 13.5 kn; Passengers: 596 in cabins, 2,400 steerage.

1854 May 1: Laid down as *Leviathan* for Eastern SN Co.

1857 Nov 3: Abortive attempt at launching. The ship moved only a few yards broadside down the slipway, then remained stuck.

1858 Jan 31: The launching succeeded on an extremely high tide. The Eastern SN Co was financially ruined because of the long building-time. The *Leviathan* was sold to the Great Ship Co and renamed *Great Eastern*. The ship, hitherto intended for service to India, was now fitted out for the North Atlantic run.

1859 Sep 7: Trials. The ship left London for Portland to take on a party of guests. Off Hastings there was a boiler explosion. Six dead. During further trials after repairs the *Great Eastern* ran into difficulties in heavy weather and was afterwards laid-up at Southampton.

1860 Jun 17: Maiden voyage Southampton–New York. The steamer remained on the North Atlantic service until 1863 but was neither popular with passengers nor successful for her owners. The giant ship would roll extraordinarily heavily in a seaway. The paddle-wheels were often damaged and on one occasion completely destroyed.

1863 Dec: Liquidation of the Great Ship Co.

1864 Feb: The newly-formed Great Eastern Co bought the ship.
Jul: The *Great Eastern* towed to Sheerness for fitting-out as a cable-layer. At this time her fourth funnel and the boiler beneath were removed.

1865 Jun 4: The new cable-layer left the Medway on charter to the Telegraph Construction & Maintenance Co and commenced the laying of an under-sea cable between Valentia and Newfoundland. After 1,000 miles the cable snapped and the undertaking was abandoned.

1866 Jul 13–26: Renewed cable-laying, Valentia–Newfoundland, which succeeded without incident. This connection was the first usable Transatlantic cable, after the first cable, laid in 1858, had failed to function after a few weeks.

1867 Overhaul and installation of a new boiler by G. Forrester & Co, Liverpool. The *Great Eastern* was given the first steam steering gear in the world. Used as a passenger ship between Brest and New York on the occasion of the Paris World Exhibition. Laid-up at Liverpool at the end of the year.

1869 The *Great Eastern* laid under-sea cables from France to the USA and from Aden to Bombay. Thereafter she was laid-up for seven years in Milford Haven.

1886 Chartered to David Lewis' Great Eastern Exhibition Co Ltd, Liverpool. Floating exhibition in Liverpool, Dublin and Greenock.

1887 Oct: Sold at auction. New owner planned to use the ship as a coal hulk at Gibraltar.
Nov: Sold to Henry Bath & Sons, Birkenhead, for breaking up.

1888 Aug 22: Last voyage from the Clyde to Birkenhead.

1889 Jan 1: Breaking up started at New Ferry on the River Mersey.

1891 Breaking up completed.

1

2

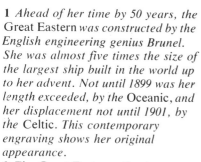

1 *Ahead of her time by 50 years, the* Great Eastern *was constructed by the English engineering genius Brunel. She was almost five times the size of the largest ship built in the world up to her advent. Not until 1899 was her length exceeded, by the* Oceanic, *and her displacement not until 1901, by the* Celtic. *This contemporary engraving shows her original appearance.*
2 The Great Eastern *after her fitting-out as a cable-layer in 1865. The fourth funnel has been removed.*

3

4

3 *A photograph of the* Great Eastern
towards the end of the 'sixties.
4 *As a 'fair-ship', shown here at
Liverpool in 1886, the* Great Eastern
*gave the impression of a floating
billboard.*

The Inman Liners

Steamship *City of New York*
Inman Line, Liverpool

1893 *New York*; 1898 *Harvard*;
1898 *New York*; 1917 *Plattsburg*;
1919 *New York*

Builders: Thomson, Glasgow
Yard no: 240
10,499 GRT; 170.7 × 19 m /
560 × 63.2 ft; III exp eng,
Thomson; Twin screw; 20,000
IHP; 20, max 21 kn; Passengers:
540 1st class, 200 2nd class, 1,000
steerage.

1888 Mar 15: Launched.
Jul 19: Delivered.
Aug 1: Maiden voyage,
Liverpool–New York.
1892 Aug: 'Blue Riband' for record voyage Sandy
Hook–Queenstown. Average
speed of 20.11 kn.
1893 Feb 22: To American Line,
New York. Renamed *New York*.
Passengers: 290 1st class, 250 2nd
class, 725 steerage. 10,508 GRT.
Mar 11: First voyage
Southampton–New York.
1898 Served briefly in US Navy
as auxiliary cruiser in the Spanish
American war, under the name of
Harvard.
1901 May: Until 1903, being
refitted by Cramp, Philadelphia.
New III exp eng. Only two
funnels. 10, 798 GRT.
1913 Passenger accommodation
rebuilt; no 1st class.
1914 Entered service on New
York–Liverpool route following
the outbreak of war.
1917 Served in US Navy until
1919 as armed transport
Plattsburg. Second mast
removed.
1919 Again *New York* of
American Line.
1920 Feb: First post-war voyage,
New York–Southampton.
Nov: laid-up.
1921 Sold to Polish Navigation
Co, New York.
Sep 14: First voyage New
York–Danzig.
1922 New York–Mediterranean
service.
1923 Broken up in Genoa.

1

1 *The* City of New York,
photographed as the New York *of
the American Line, was the first
twin-screw express steamer in the
world, and excepting the* Great
Eastern *the first of over 10,000 GRT.
In 1893, the Inman Line had to
dispense with her service because of
financial difficulties.*

Steamship *City of Paris*
Inman Line, Liverpool

1893 *Paris*; 1898 *Yale*;
1898 *Paris*; 1901 *Philadelphia*;
1917 *Harrisburg*;
1919 *Philadelphia*

Builders: Thomson, Glasgow
Yard no: 241
10,499 GRT; 170.7 × 19.0 m /
560 × 63.2 ft; III exp eng,
Thomson; Twin screw; 20,000
IHP; 20, max 21.9 kn;
Passengers: 540 1st class, 200 2nd
class, 1,000 steerage.

1888 Oct 20: Launched.
1889 Mar: Completed.
Apr 3: Maiden voyage
Liverpool–New York.
May: 'Blue Riband' for record
voyage Queenstown–Sandy
Hook (19.95 kn) and in the
opposite direction (20.02 kn
average). *City of Paris* broke the
westward record in Sep 1889,
with 20.01 kn, and again in Oct
1892 with 20.07 kn.
1890 Mar 25: The starboard
propeller shaft broke at high
speed. The racing engine was
completely wrecked and caused a
leak which put the port engine out
of action also. The ship was
towed into Queenstown and was
out of service for several months.
1893 Feb: Renamed *Paris* for the
American Line.
Mar 25: First voyage
Southampton–New York,
Passenger accommodation: 290
1st class, 250 2nd class, 725
steerage. 10,508 GRT.
1898 Served briefly in US Navy
as auxiliary cruiser in the
Spanish-American war, under the
name of *Yale*.

1899 May 21: *Paris* ran aground
on the Manacles off Cornwall.
Jul 11: Refloated by Liverpool
Salvage Association. After
provisional repairs in Falmouth
and Milford Haven lasting five
months she was sent to Belfast for
refitting by Harland & Wolff.
New IV exp engines from
Harland & Wolff, 2 funnels;
10,786 GRT.
1901 Aug 31: Re-entered service
as *Philadelphia*.
1913 Only 2nd class and steerage.
1914 Entered service on
New York–Liverpool route
following the outbreak of war.
1917 Served in US Navy until
1919 as armed transport
Harrisburg. Second mast
removed.
1919 Again *Philadelphia* of
American Line.
1920 Mar: Again on
North-Atlantic service.
Nov: Laid up.
1922 Sold to New York–Naples
SS Co, New York.
Jul 1: First voyage New
York–Naples during which a
mutiny broke out on board.
Mutineers tried to sink the ship.
Laid up on arrival in Naples.
1923 Broken up in Genoa.

2

3

2/3 *The* City of Paris *photographed
as the* Philadelphia *of the American
Line after her refit of 1901. Between
1901 and 1903 her sister ship, the*
New York, *was similarly refitted and
the number of her funnels reduced to
two.*

Campania and Lucania

Steamship *Campania*
Cunard Line, Liverpool

Builders: Fairfield, Glasgow
Yard no: 364
12,950 GRT; 188.6 × 19.9 m /
622 × 65.2 ft; III exp eng,
Fairfield; Twin screw; 30,000
IHP; 21, max 23.2 kn;
Passengers: 600 1st class, 400 2nd
class, 1,000 steerage; Crew: 415.

1892 Sep 8: Launched.
1893 Apr 13: Delivered.
Apr 22: Maiden voyage
Liverpool–New York.
May: 'Blue Riband' for record
voyage Sandy
Hook–Queenstown with average
speed of 21.9 kn. In August, 1894,
the *Campania* gained the
westbound record with a speed of
21.49 kn.
1900 Travelling at 10 kn, she
collided with the barque
Embleton in thick fog in St
George's Channel in the Irish
Sea. The latter was sliced into
two and sank, 11 dead.

1914 Oct: Sold to T. W. Ward for
breaking up.
Nov 27: British Admiralty bought
the ship and had her re-built as an
aircraft-carrier by Cammell,
Laird & Co, Birkenhead.
1916 Apr: Entered service as
HMS *Campania*.
1918 Nov 5: The *Campania's*
anchor chain broke in a storm in
the Firth of Forth. The ship was
driven against the projecting
forefoot of HMS *Revenge,* and
was so badly damaged that she
sank.

1/2 In 1916 the Cunarder Campania
*(2) was re-built as an aircraft-carrier
and sank in 1918 after a collision in
the Firth of Forth (photo 1).*

1

2

Steamship *Lucania*
Cunard Line, Liverpool

Builders: Fairfield, Glasgow
Yard no: 365
12,952 GRT; 188.6 × 19.9 m /
622 × 65.2 ft; III exp eng,
Fairfield; Twin screw; 30,000
IHP; 21, max 23 kn; Passengers:
600 1st class, 400 2nd class, 1,000
steerage; Crew: 415.

1893 Feb 2: Launched.
Aug: Completed. Until 1897 the
largest ship in the world.
Sep 2: Maiden voyage
Liverpool–New York.
Oct: 'Blue Riband' for record
voyage Queenstown–Sandy
Hook with an average speed of
20.75 kn. Further record voyages:
Oct, 1894, 21.81 kn on the same
run. In May 1894 the *Lucania*
broke the record in the other
direction with an average speed of
21.95 kn.
1909 Aug 14: Burnt out in
Liverpool. The wreck was sold
for scrap in Swansea.

3 *In 1909 the* Lucania *was destroyed
by fire in Liverpool.*

3

16 St Louis and St Paul

Steamship *St Louis*
American Line, New York

1917 *Louisville*; 1920 *St Louis*

Builders: Cramp, Philadelphia
Yard no: 277
11,629 GRT; 168.8 × 19.2 m /
554 × 63.0 ft; IV exp eng, Cramp;
Twin screw; 20,000 IHP; 19, max
22 kn; Passengers: 320 1st class,
220 2nd class, 800 steerage; Crew:
400.

1894 Nov 12: Launched.
1895 May: Completed.
Jun 5: Maiden-voyage New
York–Southampton.
Aug 1: Steam-pipe explosion, 5
dead.
1896 Jan: Overhaul of
unsatisfactory engine layout.
Removal of original funnel-tops.
1898 Jun: Served as auxiliary
cruiser and transport for duration
of Spanish-American war.
1903 Boiler damage on
Southampton–New York voyage
— speed reduced to 9 kn. New
boilers fitted by Cramp. Funnels
lengthened.
1917 Taken over by US Navy as
armed transport, renamed
Louisville.
1920 Back to American Line as
St Louis. During refitting as
passenger ship she caught fire and
sank. Raised and laid-up.

1922 The Anderson Overseas
Corp, New York, bought the ship
and planned to fit her out as a
cruise liner. Plans not realised.
1924 Jan: Sold for breaking up to
E. & S. Casano, Genoa.
May 20: Towed by the *Zwarte
Zee*, the *St Louis* left New York
for Genoa on her last voyage.

Steamship *St Paul*
American Line, New York

1918 *Knoxville*; 1920 *St Paul*

Builders: Cramp, Philadelphia
Yard no: 278
11,629 GRT; 168.8 × 19.2 m /
554 × 63.0 ft; IV exp eng, Cramp;
Twin screw; 20,000 IHP; 19, max
21 kn; Passengers: 350 1st class,
220 2nd class, 800 steerage; Crew:
400.

1895 Mar 25: The launching,
planned for this day, had to be
postponed because of a faulty
slipway.
Apr 9: Launched.
Oct 4: Delivered.
Oct 9: Maiden voyage New
York–Southampton.
Sent back to shipyard at end of
year for improvement of hitherto

unsatisfactory speed. Funnel-tops
removed during reconstruction.
1898 Apr: auxiliary cruiser for
duration of Spanish-American
war.
1900 Nov: Collision with
submerged wreck. Starboard
propeller lost, racing engine
completely wrecked.
1907 New boilers fitted, funnels
lengthened.
1908 Apr 25: Collided with
British cruiser *Gladiator* off
Southampton. The latter sank
with the loss of 27 lives.
1913 Passenger accommodation
for 2nd class and steerage only.
1914 On New York–Liverpool
route following the outbreak of
war.
1918 Fitting-out commenced as
armed transport for US Navy.
Renamed *Knoxville*.
Apr 25: Capsized in New York
before completion of fitting-out.
1920 Mar: After repairs, back to
American Line as *St Paul*. North
Atlantic service to various
European ports.
1923 Jul: Laid up.
Oct 19: Arrival at the naval
dockyard at Wilhelmshaven in
tow of the *Jacob van Heemskerk*,
for breaking-up.

1 *When, in 1893, the American Line wanted to buy the two Inman liners, they had to ask Congress for special dispensation from the regulation that allowed only American-built ships to fly the American flag. The shipping line got the dispensation on condition that they ordered two equivalent ships in the USA. The* St Louis *was the first of these.*

2 *In 1899 the* St Paul *was the first commercial vessel to be fitted with radio.*

3 *The capsized transport* Knoxville *(ex* St Paul*) in New York in 1918.*

The Barbarossa Class

Steamship *Friedrich der Grosse*
North German Lloyd, Bremen

1917 *Huron;*
1922 *City of Honolulu*

Builders: 'Vulcan', Stettin
Yard no: 231
10,531 GRT; 166.4 × 18.3 m /
546 × 60.1 ft; IV exp eng,
Vulcan; Twin screw; 8,000 IHP;
14.4, max 15.2 kn; Passengers:
216 1st class, 243 2nd class, 1,964
steerage; Crew: 222.

1896 Aug 1: Launched.
Nov 11: Completed.
Nov: Maiden voyage
Bremerhaven–Australia.
Used on North Atlantic or
Australian services as required.
Also Mediterranean–New York
from 1907.
1902 10,696 GRT after
reconstruction.
1914 Aug: Interned in New
York.
1917 Apr 6: Seized by US Navy.
Renamed *Huron*. Troop
transport.
1919 Taken over by US Shipping
Board. Fitted to burn oil fuel by
Morse, Brooklyn.
1922 Chartered to Los Angeles
Steamship Co. Renamed *City of
Honolulu* Hawaian service.
Oct 12: Caught fire 400 miles from
Los Angeles on return voyage
from Honolulu. The ship had to
be abandoned.
Oct 17: The US transport *Thomas*
sank the burnt-out wreck.

Steamship *Barbarossa*
North German Lloyd, Bremen

1917 *Mercury*

Builders: Blohm & Voss,
Hamburg
Yard no: 115
10,769 GRT; 167.1 × 18.3 m /
548 × 60.1 ft; IV exp eng, B & V;
Twin screw; 8,000 IHP; 14.5,
max 15.3 kn; Passengers: 230 1st
class, 227 2nd class, 1,935
steerage; Crew: 226.

1896 Sep 5: Launched.
1897 Jan 3: Completed.
Jan 8: Maiden-voyage
Bremerhaven–Australia.
Used for both North Atlantic and
Australian service.
1902 10,915 GRT, after
reconstruction.
1914 Aug: Interned in New
York.
1917 Apr 6: Seized by US Navy
and used as transport. Renamed
Mercury.
1919 Taken over by US Shipping
board.
1920 Jul: Chartered to Baltic SS
Corp of America for New
York–Danzig service. Never
made voyage due to liquidation of
shippping line.
1921 Laid up.
1924 Broken up in USA.

1 *Steamship* Friedrich der Grosse
the first German 10,000 tonner.
2 *The* Huron, *ex-*Friedrich der
Grosse, *in 1920.*
3 *The steamship* Barbarossa, *the
name-ship of the class.*

1

2

3

Steamship *Königin Luise*
North German Lloyd, Bremen

1921 *Omar*; 1924 *Edison*

Builders: 'Vulcan', Stettin
Yard no: 232
10,566 GRT; 168.3 × 18.3 m /
552 × 60.2 ft; IV exp eng,
Vulcan; Twin screw; 8,000 IHP;
14.5, max 15 kn; Passengers: 225
1st class, 235 2nd class, 1,940
steerage; Crew: 231.

1896 Oct 17: Launched.
1897 Mar 16: Completed.
Mar 22: Maiden-voyage
Bremerhaven–New York. Used
for both North Atlantic and
Australian service. Between 1904
and 1914, Mediterranean–New
York.
1902 10,711 after reconstruction.
1910 *Königin Luise* rescued 19
men from the sinking British
sailing ship *Harvard Queen*.
1912 Reconstructed. 10,785
GRT.
1919 Apr 10: Handed over to
Great Britain. Managed by the
Orient SN Co for the Shipping
controller.
1920 Sep 4: First voyage
London–Australia. 11,103 GRT
Sep 8: *Königin Luise* collided in
Lisbon with the British steamship
Loughborough which
immediately sank.
1921 Jan: Purchased by Orient
SN Co, London. Renamed
Omar.
1924 Jul: Sold to Byron SS Co,
London. Renamed *Edison*.
Piraeus–New York service.
1929 Registered in Piraeus for
National SN Co of Greece, an
associate of the Byron SS Co.
1935 Broken up in Italy.

4

5

4 *Steamship* Königin Luise *after reconstruction in 1912.*
5 *The* Edison *ex-*Königin Luise, *was used on the Piraeus–New York service.*

Steamship *Bremen*
North German Lloyd, Bremen

1921 *Constantinople;* 1923 *King Alexander*

Builders: Schichau, Danzig
Yard no: 583
10,552 GRT; 167.6 × 18.4 m /
550 × 60.2 ft; IV exp eng,
Schichau; Twin screw; 7,900
IHP; 14.5, max 15.5 kn;
Passengers: 230 1st class, 250 2nd
class, 1,850 steerage; Crew: 250.

1896 Nov 14: Launched.
1897 May 26: Completed.
Jun 5: Maiden-voyage
Bremerhaven–New York; used
for both North Atlantic and
Australian services.
1900 Jun 30: A fire broke out on
the NGL pier at Hoboken (New
York) through the spontaneous
combustion of a bale of cotton. It
spread quickly through all the
buildings and to the Lloyd ships
Saale, Main, Kaiser Wilhelm der Grosse and the *Bremen*. Tugs
towed the burning ships out into
open water. The *Saale* was
completely burnt out. The *Main*
and the *Bremen* ran aground,
severely damaged. The disaster
claimed nearly 300 lives,
including some of the courageous
tugboat men. There were 12 dead
from the *Bremen.*
Oct 11: Sailed for home after
temporary repairs. Repaired and
refitted by 'Vulcan', Stettin.
1901 Oct: In service again; now
11,540 GRT; 175.3 m / 575 ft
length overall.
1905 Sep: During voyage from
New York to Bremen the port
propeller shaft broke. Starboard
propeller unusable at same time.
The tanker *Lucigen* towed the
disabled *Bremen* into Halifax.
1908 Dec: The *Bremen* took 600
refugees from Messina to Naples
after Etna had erupted.
1919 Apr 4: Handed over to
Great Britain. Managed by P & O
Line, London, for the Shipping
Controller. Australian service.
1921 Sold to Byron SN Co,
London. Renamed
Constantinople. Piraeus–New
York service.
1924 Renamed *King Alexander.*
1929 Broken up in Italy.

7

*7 The fire disaster in New York on
June 30, 1900. Tugs towed the*
Bremen *(left) and the* Main *away
from the danger zone.*

6 *The* Bremen *after the refit of 1901.*
8 *After the First World War, the*
Bremen, *renamed* King Alexander,
sailed under the British flag.

Steamship *König Albert*
North German Lloyd, Bremen

1915 *Ferdinando Palasciano;*
1923 *Italia*

Builders: 'Vulcan', Stettin
Yard no: 242
10,643 GRT; 158.6 × 18.3 m /
521 × 60.2 ft; IV exp eng,
Vulcan; Twin screw; 9,000 IHP;
15.3, max 16 kn; Passengers: 257
1st class, 119 2nd class, 1,799
steerage; Crew: 230.

1899 Jun 24: Launched.
Sep 27: Completed.
Oct 4: Maiden voyage
Bremerhaven–Yokohama.
1903 Mar 13: First voyage
Bremerhaven–New York; from
1905 mainly on
Mediterranean–New York
service.
1914 Aug: Interned in Italy.
1915 May 25: Seized in Genoa.
Renamed *Ferdinando
Palasciano*; served as hospital
ship.
1920 Navigazione Generale
Italiana, Genoa, bought the ship
from the Italian government.
Jun 15: First voyage Genoa–New
York.
1923 Renamed *Italia*. Served as
transport for the Navy.
1925 Laid up.
1926 Broken up in Italy.

Steamship *Hamburg*
Hamburg-America Line,
Hamburg

1914 *Red Cross;*
1914 *Hamburg*; 1917 *Powhatan*;
1920 *New Rochelle*; 1921 *Hudson*;
1922 *President Fillmore*

Builders: 'Vulcan', Stettin
Yard no: 243
10,532 GRT; 158.5 × 18.3 m /
521 × 60.2 ft; IV exp eng,
Vulcan; Twin screw; 9,000 IHP;
15.3, max 16 kn; Passengers: 290
1st class, 100 2nd class, 80 3rd
class, 1,700 steerage; Crew: 225.

1899 Nov 25: Launched. Until
Oct 1899, her intended name had
been *Bavaria*.
1900 Mar 12: Completed. Maiden
voyage, Hamburg–Far East.
1903 Oct 30: Rescued the 17-man
crew of a Chinese fishing boat.
1904 Jun 2: First voyage
Hamburg–New York; from 1906
used also in Genoa–New York
service.
1910 Feb 27: The tugboat *Eolo*
collided with the *Hamburg* in
Naples harbour and sank.
1914 Aug: Interned in New
York.
Sep: Chartered to the US Red
Cross; renamed *Red Cross*.
Sep 13: Voyage from New York
to Rotterdam.
Oct 23: In New York again.

Renamed *Hamburg*.
1917 Apr 6: Seized, renamed
Powhatan. Hospital ship with US
Navy.
1919 To US Shipping Board.
1920 Aug 5: First voyage New
York–Danzig on charter to the
Baltic SS Corp of America, under
the name of *New Rochelle*.
1921 Feb 11: First voyage New
York–Danzig on charter to the
US Mail SS Co.
May: Renamed *Hudson*.
Aug: New York–Bremen service
on charter to United States Lines.
1922 Jul: Renamed *President
Fillmore*.
1924 To the Dollar Line, San
Francisco. Round the World
service.
1928 Sold for breaking up in the
USA.

9 König Albert *was the first ship in
the somewhat faster second series of
the* Barbarossa *class.*
10 *Until shortly before launching, the*
Hamburg, *pictured here, was
intended by the Hamburg-America
Line to be named* Bavaria.
11 *Kaiser Wilhelm II used the*
Hamburg *twice as a state yacht for
foreign visits, for each of which
occasions the ship received a coat of
white paint.*

9

10

11

Steamship *Grosser Kurfürst*
North German Lloyd, Bremen

1917 *Aeolus*; 1922 *City of Los Angeles*

Builders: Schichau, Danzig
Yard no: 643
13,182 GRT; 177.1 × 19.0 m / 581 × 62.3 ft; III exp eng, Schichau; Twin screw; 9,700 IHP; 15, max 16 kn; Passengers: 299 1st class, 317 2nd class, 172 3rd class, 2,201 steerage; Crew: 273.

1899 Dec 2: Launched.
1900 Apr 26: Completed.
May 5: Maiden voyage Bremerhaven–New York.
Nov 7: First voyage Bremerhaven–Australia. Used for both New York and Australian service.
1913 Oct 9: The British steamship *Volturno,* on fire in mid-Atlantic with 600 emigrants on board, sent out a distress call. The *Grosser Kurfürst* and eight other ships steamed to the rescue. These included the *Seydlitz* of NGL, the *Carmania* of Cunard, *Kroonland* of the Red Star Line, the Atlantic Transport liner *Minneapolis,* the *La Touraine* of CGT, the Russian *Czar* and the British tanker *Narragansett.* The next morning, after the *Narragansett* had calmed the sea by pumping out oil, 521 survivors were rescued.
1914 Aug: Interned in New York.
1917 Apr 6: Seized. Renamed *Aeolus,* and used as transport by US Navy.
1919 Sep: Handed over to US Shipping Board.

1920 Feb: Chartered to Munson Line, New York. Alterations to passenger accommodation in Baltimore. Converted to oil-firing. On Sep 10 four killed in an explosion in the course of installation.
Dec 1: First voyage New York–La Plata.
1922 Mar: The *Aeolus* rammed the British freighter *Zero* in the South Atlantic and took her crew on board. The *Zero* sank.
Jun: Chartered to Los Angeles SS Co. Renamed *City of Los Angeles*.
Sep 11: First voyage Los Angeles–Honolulu.
1923 Sep: The Los Angeles SS Co bought the Ship from the US Shipping Board, and, despite her age, had her fitted-out by the Bethlehem Shipbuilding Corp, Quincy, as a luxury liner for 446 1st class passengers. New turbines. 11,000 SHP; 17 kn; 12,642 GRT.
1924 Jun: Again on Hawaii service.
1932 Laid-up because of the world economic depression.
1933 The Matson Line, San Francisco, bought the Los Angeles SS Co. After a few voyages for her new owners, the *City of Los Angeles* was laid up in San Diego.
1937 Feb: Sailed to Japan for breaking-up.

12 *The* Grosser Kurfürst, *the largest ship of the Barbarossa class.*
13 *The* City of Los Angeles *ex-*Grosser Kurfürst, *after refitting in 1923.*

Steamship *Prinzess Irene*
North German Lloyd, Bremen

1917 *Pocahontas*; 1923 *Bremen*;
1928 *Karlsruhe*

Builders: 'Vulcan', Stettin
Yard no: 245
10,881 GRT; 164.6 × 18.3 m /
540 × 60.2 ft; IV exp eng,
Vulcan; Twin screw; 9,000 IHP;
15.2, max 16 kn; Passengers: 268
1st class, 132 2nd class, 1,954
steerage; Crew: 230.

1900 Jun 19: Launched.
Sep 6: Completed.
Sep 9: Maiden voyage
Bremerhaven–New York.
Nov 3: First voyage
Bremerhaven–Far East.
1903 Apr 30: Rescued crew of the
sinking Austrian schooner
Marije.
1909 Jun 10: *Prinzess Irene* took
110 people on board from the
Cunard steamship *Slavonia*,
which had stranded off the
Azores.
1914 Aug: Interned in New
York.
1917 Apr 6: Seized. Renamed
Pocahontas, and used by US
Navy as transport.
1919 Handed over to US
Shipping Board.
1920 Chartered to United States
Mail SS Co, New York.
1921 Feb 26: First voyage New
York–Italy. After only a few
voyages the *Pocahontas* had to
remain in Gibraltar with
machinery damage. The shipping
company went into liquidation.
1922 Sep: North German Lloyd
bought the ship back. She was
towed to Bremerhaven, where
she was repaired and refitted.
10,826 GRT.

1923 Renamed *Bremen*.
Apr 7: First voyage
Bremerhaven–New York.
1926 Jan 26: In a highly dramatic
rescue operation she managed to
save six men from the British
freighter *Laristan*, sinking in a
snowstorm in the Atlantic. The
Laristan went down during the
night of Jan 27 with 26 of her crew
still aboard.
1928 Jan: Renamed *Karlsruhe*.
1932 Broken up in Germany.

Steamship *Kiautschou*
Hamburg–America Line,
Hamburg

1904 *Prinzess Alice*; 1917 *Princess
Matoika*; 1922 *President Arthur*;
1927 *City of Honolulu*

Builders: 'Vulcan', Stettin
Yard no: 246
10,911 GRT; 164.6 × 18.3 m /
540 × 60.2 ft; IV exp eng,
Vulcan; Twin screw; 9,000 IHP;
15.2, max 16 kn; Passengers: 327
1st class, 103 2nd class, 80 3rd
class, 1,700 steerage; Crew: 230.

1900 Sep 14: Launched. Intended
as *Borussia* until Oct 1899, then
as *Teutonia* until Nov 1899.
Dec 14: Completed.
Dec: Maiden voyage,
Hamburg–Far East service.
1904 Feb: Sold to North German
Lloyd, Bremen; renamed
Prinzess Alice. Bremerhaven–Far
East service.
1914 Aug: Interned in Manila.
1917 Apr 6: Seized by US
Shipping Board, renamed
Princess Matoika.
1918 US Navy transport.
1919 Handed back to US
Shipping Board.

1920 Chartered to US Mail SS
Co. 10,421 GRT after
re-construction.
1921 Jan 19: First voyage New
York–Genoa. Later, New
York–Danzig.
Aug: Chartered to United States
Lines; New York–Bremerhaven
service.
1922 Renamed *President Arthur*.
1923 Laid up.
1925 Sold to American Palestine
Line, New York. Intended for
New York–Mediterranean
service, under the name of *White
Palace*, but sold again at the end
of 1925 to C. L. Dimon, New
York.
1926 Acquired by the Los
Angeles SS Co. Fitted out as
luxury liner at the San Pedro
shipyard of the Los Angeles
Shipbuilding & Dry Dock Corp.
10,860 GRT. Passengers: 445 1st
class, 50 3rd class. With new
boilers, the engines gave 11,000
IHP at 17 kn.
1927 Jun: Renamed *City of
Honolulu*, Los Angeles–Hawaii
service.
1930 May 25: Burnt out in
Honolulu. Back to Los Angeles
without passengers and laid up.
1933 Aug: Sold to shipbreakers at
Osaka.

14 *The* Karlsruhe, *built in 1900 as the*
Prinzess Irene, *photographed as a
cruise liner.*
15 *The* Kiautschou *was used by
Hamburg-America Line, for their Far
East service, until she was sold to
North German Lloyd in 1904.*
16 *Refitting to become the* City of
Honolulu *considerably altered the
appearance of the former*
Kiautschou.

14

15

16

Steamship *Moltke*
Hamburg-America Line,
Hamburg

1915 *Pesaro*

Builders: Blohm & Voss,
Hamburg
Yard no: 150
12,335 GRT; 167.5 × 18.9 m /
550 × 60.2 ft; IV exp eng, B & V;
Twin screw; 9,900 IHP; 16, max
16.5 kn; Passengers: 333 1st class;
169 2nd class; 1,600 steerage;
Crew: 252.

1901 Aug 27: Launched.
1902 Feb 22: Completed.
Mar 9: Maiden voyage
Hamburg–New York.
1906 Apr 3: Genoa–New York
service.
1914 Aug: Interned in Genoa.
1915 May 25: Seized by Italian
government, renamed *Pesaro*.
Managed by Italian State
Railways.
1919 To Lloyd Sabaudo,
Genoa–New York service.
1925 Broken up in Italy.

Steamship *Blücher*
Hamburg-America Line,
Hamburg

1917 *Leopoldina*; 1923 *Suffren*

Builders: Blohm & Voss,
Hamburg
Yard no: 151
12,334 GRT; 167.5 × 18.9 m /
550 × 62.0 ft; IV exp eng, B & V;
Twin screw; 9,900 IHP; 16, max
16.7 kn; Passengers: 333 1st class,
169 2nd class, 1,600 steerage;
Crew: 252.

1901 Nov 23: Launched.
1902 May 31: Completed.
Jun 6: Maiden voyage
Hamburg–New York.
1912 Hamburg–South America
service.
1914 Aug: Interned in
Pernambuco.
1917 Jun 1: Seized by Brazilian
government; renamed
Leopoldina.
1919 Handed over to French
government.
1920 Mar: Chartered to CGT, Le
Havre, Le Havre–New York
service.
1921 Dec: Laid up.
1923 Mar: Sold to CGT,
renamed *Suffren*.
May 8: First voyage Le
Havre–New York. Passengers:
500 2nd class, 250 3rd class.
1929 May: Broken up in Genoa.

17/18 *The sister-ships* Moltke *(17)* *and* Blücher *were planned for use on Far East service, but sailed only on the Atlantic.*

The P-Class of the Hamburg-America Line

Steamer *Pennsylvania*
Hamburg-America Line,
Hamburg

1917 *Nansemond*

Builders: Harland & Wolff,
Belfast
Yard no: 302
12,891 GRT; 176.5 × 18.9 m /
579 × 62.2 ft; IV exp eng, H & W;
Twin screw; 5,400 IHP ; 13 kn;
Passengers: 162 1st class, 180 2nd
class, 2,382 steerage; Crew 250.

1896 Sep 10: Launched.
1897 Jan 30: Maiden voyage
Belfast–New York.
Mar 22: First voyage
Hamburg–New York.
1900 Remeasured: 13,333 GRT.
1902 Sep 24: Rescued crew of the
sinking Norwegian barque
Bothnia. The 13 men had battled
for 17 days against rising water.
1910 Mar 8: The *Pennsylvania*
rammed the Hamburg schooner
Gertrud, which had suddenly
strayed off course in the mouth of
the Elbe. The schooner sank
immediately, and of the six-man
crew only one could be saved.
Passenger accommodation: 404
2nd class, 2,200 steerage.
1914 Aug: Interned in New
York.
1917 Apr 6: Seized. Renamed
Nansemond and used as transport
by US Navy.
1919 Handed over to US
Shipping Board and laid up in the
Hudson.
1924 Broken up.

Steamship *Pretoria*
Hamburg-America Line,
Hamburg

Builders: Blohm & Voss,
Hamburg
Yard no: 123
12,800 GRT; 178.6 × 18.9 m /
586 × 62.0 ft; IV exp eng, B & V;
Twin screw; 5,360 IHP; 13 kn;
Passengers: 162 1st class, 197 2nd
class, 2,382 steerage; Crew: 249.

1897 Oct 9: Launched.
1898 Feb 8: Completed.
Feb 15: Maiden voyage
Hamburg–New York.
1900 Re-measured: 13,234 GRT.
1908 Oct 9: Collided in thick fog
near Texel with the Stettin
steamer *Nipponia* which sank
with the loss of all hands.
1910 Passengers: 400 2nd class,
2,200 steerage.
1919 Mar 24: Handed over to
USA for use as Army transport.
1920 Sep 10: Handed over to
British Government. Managed
for the Shipping Controller by
Ellerman Lines, Liverpool.
1921 Nov: Sold for breaking-up.

1 *The* Pennsylvania *of
Hamburg-America Line. The
flight-deck visible in the photograph
was fitted in 1910. In November of
that year, an attempt was to have
been made at launching an aircraft
from this platform at a distance of 50
nautical miles from the mainland.
However, due to bad weather
conditions, the attempt was not
made. After later tests by the Navy,
the flight deck was removed.*
2 Nansemond *ex-*Pennsylvania *at St
Nazaire in 1918.*
3 *The* Pretoria.

1

2

3

Steamship *Graf Waldersee*
Hamburg America Line,
Hamburg

Builders: Blohm & Voss,
Hamburg
Yard no: 131
12,830 GRT; 178.6 × 18.9 m /
586 × 62.0 ft; IV exp eng, B & V;
Twin screw; 5,400 IHP; 13 kn;
Passengers: 162 1st class, 184 2nd
class, 2,200 steerage; Crew: 250.

1898 Dec 10: Launched.
Intended name *Pavia*.
1899 Mar 18: Completed.
Apr 2: Maiden voyage,
Hamburg–New York.
1900 Remeasured: 13,193 GRT.
1910 Passengers: 408 2nd class,
2,300 steerage.
1919 Mar 23: Handed over to
USA for use as US Navy
transport.
1920 Handed over to British
Government. Managed for the
Shipping Controller by P & O
Line, London.
1921 Aug 10: Sold by auction to
T. W. Ward.
Sep: Resold to the Köhlbrand
yard in Hamburg for breaking-up.
1922 Broken up.

Steamship *Patricia*
Hamburg-America Line,
Hamburg

Builders: 'Vulcan', Stettin
Yard no: 241
13,023 GRT; 178.3 × 18.9 m /
585 × 62.4 ft; IV exp eng,
Vulcan; Twin screw; 5,460 IHP;
13 kn; Passengers: 162 1st class,
184 2nd class, 2,143 steerage;
Crew: 249.

1899 Feb 20: Launched.
May 30: Completed.
Jun 7: Maiden voyage
Hamburg–New York.
1900 Remeasured: 13,424 GRT.
1910 Jan 2: Collided in fog with
the *Elbe V*. The lightship sank,
but the crew were rescued.
Remeasured: 14,472 GRT 400
2nd class, 2,100 steerage.
1919 Mar 22: Handed over to
USA for use as US Navy
transport.
1920 Handed over to the British
Shipping Controller; managed by
Ellerman Lines, Liverpool.
1921 Broken up in England.

4 *The* Graf Waldersee *was completed by Blohm & Voss in 1899.*
5 *As last ship of the P-Class, the* Patricia *entered service in 1899.*
6 *The* Patricia *in 1920 as an Ellerman liner.*

4

Union Line and Union-Castle Line

Steamship *Briton*
Union Steam Ship Co Ltd,
Southampton

Builders: Harland & Wolff,
Belfast
Yard no: 313
10,248 GRT; 167.1 × 18.4 m /
549 × 60.3 ft; III exp eng, H & W;
Twin screw; 10,500 IHP; 17 kn;
Passengers: 260 1st class, 192
2nd class, 186 3rd class, approx
300 steerage as required; Crew:
230.

1897 Jun 5: Launched.
Nov: Completed.
Dec 4: Maiden voyage
Southampton–Cape Town.
1900 Feb: The Union Line and
the Castle Line merged to form
the Union-Castle Steam Ship Co
Ltd.
1914 The *Briton* served for a
short time as a troop transport. At
the end of 1914 she returned to
civilian Africa service, but after a
year returned to serve once again
as a troop transport.
1920 First post-war voyage in
Southampton–South Africa
passenger service.
1925 Jan: Laid up as reserve ship.
In service again from October to
November.
1926 Apr: Sold for breaking-up in
Italy.

Steamship *Saxon*
Union Steam Ship Co Ltd,
Southampton

Builders: Harland & Wolff,
Belfast
Yard no: 326
12,970 GRT; 178.6 × 19.6 m /
586 × 64.4 ft; IV exp eng, H & W;
Twin screw; 12,000 IHP; 17.5,
max 18.25 kn; Passengers: 310 1st
class, 203 2nd class, 286 3rd class;
Crew: 250.

1899 Dec 21: Launched.
1900 Feb: Merger of Union SS
Co and Castle Line as
Union-Castle Line.
May: Completed.
Jun 16: Maiden voyage
Southampton–Cape Town.
1917 Jan: The *Saxon* became a
troop transport.
1919 First post-war voyage in
South Africa passenger service.
1931 Jun: Laid up in
Southampton.
1935 Sold for breaking-up to
Hughes, Bolckow & Co, Blyth.

1 *The* Briton *in her early years of
service, still in the colours of the
Union Line.*
2 *The* Saxon, *placed in service
shortly before the merger between the
Union Line and the Castle Line, was
a development of the* Briton *and the
prototype of the Union-Castle
express steamers built up to the First
World War.*

Steamship *Walmer Castle*
Union-Castle Line, London

Builders: Harland & Wolff,
Belfast
Yard no: 342
12,546 GRT; 175.6 × 19.6 m /
576 × 64.4 ft; IV exp eng, H & W;
Twin screw; 12,000 IHP; 17.5 kn;
Passengers: 336 1st class, 174 2nd
class, 244 3rd class; Crew: 250.

1901 Jul 6: Launched. Laid down
before the merger as *Celt* for the
Union Line.
1902 Jan: Completed.
Mar 15: Maiden voyage
Southampton–Cape Town.
1917 Taken over by British
Shipping Controller and entered
service in 1918 as troop transport.
1919 Returned to
Southampton–South Africa
passenger service.
1930 Laid up in Southampton.
1931 Dec: Sold for breaking-up
to Hughes, Bolckow & Co.
1932 Feb: The *Walmer Castle*
left Southampton for Blyth on her
last voyage.

Steamship *Armadale Castle*
Union-Castle Line, London

Builders: Fairfield, Glasgow
Yard no: 424
12,973 GRT; 179.9 × 19.6 m /
590.1 × 64.4 ft; IV exp eng,
Fairfield; Twin screw; 12,500
IHP; 17 kn; Passengers: 350 1st
class, 200 2nd class, 270 3rd class;
Crew: 260.

1903 Aug 11: Launched.
Nov 16: Delivered.
Dec 5: Maiden voyage
Southampton–Cape Town.
1914 Aug 7: Auxiliary cruiser
with the 10th cruiser Squadron, at
the same time troop transport.
1918 Released from naval
service, returned to South Africa
passenger service.
1935 Laid up.
1936 Broken up.

Steamship *Kenilworth Castle*
Union-Castle Line, London

Builders: Harland & Wolff,
Belfast
Yard no: 356
12,975 GRT; 179.9 × 19.7 m /
590 × 64.7 ft; IV exp eng, H & W;
Twin screws; 12,500 IHP; 17 kn;
Passengers: 340 1st class, 200 2nd
class, 270 3rd class; Crew: 260.

1903 Dec 15: Launched.
May: Completed.
Southampton–Cape Town
Service.
1936 Broken up.

3

3/4 The Walmer Castle, *seen in photo 4 in camouflage paint as a troop transport in 1918.*
5 The Armadale Castle *in the 'twenties with glass-enclosed bridge.*
6 The Kenilworth Castle *and Table Mountain, Cape Town.*

4

5

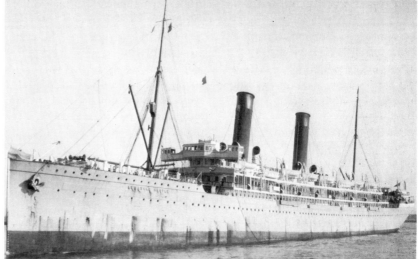

6

Nine White Star Liners

Steamship *Cymric*
White Star Line, Liverpool

Builders: Harland & Wolff,
Belfast
Yard no: 316
12,552 GRT; 182.6 × 19.5 m /
599 × 64.3 ft; IV exp eng, H & W;
Twin screw; 6,800 IHP; 14.5 kn;
Passengers: 258 1st class, 1,160
steerage.

1897 Oct 12: Launched.
1898 Feb 5: Delivered.
Feb 11: Maiden voyage
Liverpool–New York.
1900 Jan: Served as transport No
74 to South Africa during Boer
War, made two round trips.
1903 Dec 10: First voyage
Liverpool–Boston.
1913 Passenger accommodation
altered. 1st class became 2nd
class.
1915 Re-entered service
Liverpool–New York.
1916 May 8: The *Cymric* was
torpedoed 140 nautical miles
north west of Fastnet by the
German submarine U 20, and
sank the following day. Five
dead.

Steamship *Afric*
White Star Line, Liverpool

Builders: Harland & Wolff,
Belfast
Yard no: 322
11,816 GRT; 173.7 × 19.3 m /
570 × 63.3 ft; IV exp eng, H & W;
Twin screw; 5,000 IHP; 13.5 kn;
Passengers: 350 cabin class.

1898 Nov 16: Launched.
1899 Feb 2: Delivered.
Feb 8: Maiden voyage
Liverpool–New York.
11,948 GRT following
re-construction by Harland &
Wolff.
Sep 9: First voyage
Liverpool–Sydney.
1917 Feb 12: The *Afric* was
torpedoed 12 nautical miles south
west of Eddystone by the German
submarine UC 66, and sank. 22
dead.

Steamship *Medic*
White Star Line, Liverpool

1928 *Hektoria*

Builders: Harland & Wolff,
Belfast
Yard no: 323
11,985 GRT; 173.7 × 19.3 m /
570 × 63.3 ft; IV exp eng, H & W;
Twin screw; 5,000 IHP; 13.5 kn;
Passengers: 320 cabin class.

1898 Dec 15: Launched.
1899 Jul 6: Delivered.
Aug 3: Maiden voyage
Liverpool–Sydney.
Sep: Troop transport during Boer
War.
1900 Jan: Returned to
commercial service.
1928 Jun: Sold to N. Bugge,
Tönsberg. Rebuilt as mother ship
for whaling fleet by Grayson,
Rollo & Clover Docks,
Birkenhead. Renamed *Hektoria*.
13,797 GRT.
1932 Sold to Hektoria Ltd,
London.
1942 Sep 12: Torpedoed and sunk
in Atlantic, position 48°55′ N –
33°38′ W, by German submarine
U 608.

4

1

2

3

1 *The* Cymric *was delivered in 1898 by Harland & Wolff for the North Atlantic service of the White Star Line.*
2 *The* Afric *was the first ship in a new series of 12,000 tonners for the White Star Line's Australian service.*
3/4 *White Star liner* Medic.

Steamship *Persic*
White Star Line, Liverpool

Builders: Harland & Wolff,
Belfast
Yard no: 325
11,973 GRT; 173.7 × 19.3 m /
570 × 63.3 ft; IV exp eng, H & W;
Twin screw; 5,000 IHP; 13.5 kn;
Passengers: 320 cabin class.

1899 Sep 7: Launched.
Nov 16: Delivered.
Dec 7: Maiden voyage
Liverpool–Sydney.
1900 Oct 26: The *Persic* rescued
the crew of the burning schooner
Madura.
1927 Jul 7: Last voyage from
Liverpool to shipbreakers at
Hendrik Ido Ambacht.

5 *The* Persic, *the third sister-ship to
the* Afric.

5

Steamship *Runic*
White Star Line, Liverpool

1930 *New Sevilla*

Builders: Harland & Wolff,
Belfast
Yard no: 332
12,482 GRT; 172.2 × 19.3 m /
565 × 63.3 ft; IV exp eng, H & W;
Twin screw; 5,000 IHP; 13.5 kn;
Passengers: 400 cabin class.

1900 Oct 25: Launched.
Dec 22: Delivered.
1901 Jan 3: Maiden voyage
Liverpool–Sydney.
1930 May: Sold to Sevilla
Whaling Co (Chr. Salvesen),
Leith. Rebuilt as whaling fleet
mother-ship at Germania
shipyard, Kiel. Renamed *New
Sevilla*. 13,801 GRT.
1940 Sep 20: Torpedoed and sunk
off Galway, position 55°48′ N –
07°22′ W, by German submarine
U 138. Two dead.

6 *The* Runic *was a slightly enlarged
version of the* Afric *class.*

6

Steamship *Suevic*
White Star Line, Liverpool

1928 *Skytteren*

Builders: Harland & Wolff,
Belfast
Yard no: 333
12,531 GRT; 172.2 × 19.3 m /
565 × 63.3 ft; IV exp eng, H & W;
Twin screw; 5,000 IHP; 13.5 kn;
Passengers: 400 cabin class.

1900 Dec 8: Launched.
1901 Mar 9: Delivered.
Mar 23: Maiden voyage
Liverpool–Sydney.
1907 Mar 17: Stranded on Stag
Rock near the Lizard and broke
into two between bridge and
second mast.
Apr: After section salvaged and
towed to Southampton. New
forward section constructed by
Harland & Wolff, built on by
Thornycroft.
1908 Jan: Re-entered service.
1920 Feb 2: First post-war
voyage in Australian service.
1921 Passenger accommodation
for 226 2nd class.
1928 Oct: Sold to Y.
Hvistendahl, Tönsberg. Rebuilt
as whaling mother-ship at
Germania Shipyard, Kiel.
Renamed *Skytteren*. 12,686 GRT.
1940 Interned in Gothenburg.
1942 Apr 1: Surprised by
German Navy in an attempt to
break through to England. The
crew of the *Skytteren* sank their
ship off Maseskjaer.

7

8

7/8 *The* Suevic, *a sister-ship to the*
Runic, *stranded in 1907 off the Lizard*
and broke in two.

Steamship *Athenic*
White Star Line, Liverpool

1928 *Pelagos*

Builders: Harland & Wolff,
Belfast
Yard no: 341
12,234 GRT; 157.1 × 19.3 m /
516 × 63.3 ft; IV exp eng, H & W;
Twin screw; 5,000 IHP; 14 kn;
Passengers; 121 1st class, 117
2nd class, 450 3rd class.

1901 Aug 17: Launched.
1902 Jan 23: Delivered.
Feb 14: Maiden voyage
London–Wellington.
1920 May 3: The *Athenic* rescued
members of the crew of the
American steamer *Munamar* in
the Pacific.
1928 May: Sold to
Hvalfangerselskapet Pelagos
A/S, (Bruun & vd Lippe)
Tönsberg. Rebuilt as whaling
mother-ship by Smith's Dock Co
at South Bank-on-Tees. Renamed
Pelagos. 12,067 GRT.
1941 Jan 15: Captured in the
Antartic by the German auxiliary
cruiser *Pinguin* and sent to
Bordeaux with a prize crew.
Managed under the German flag
by Erste Deutsche
Walfang-Gesellschaft. Used as
experimental vessel by the 24th
U-Boat Flotilla in Norway.
1944 Oct 24: Sunk at Kirkenes.
1945 Raised by the Norwegians
after the war. After repairs,
served as a whaler again.
1962 Jun 28: Arrived in
Hamburg. Broken up by Eckardt
& Co.

9

10

9 *The White Star Line had the three
sister-ships* Athenic, Corinthic *and*
Ionic *built for their New Zealand
service.*
10 *The whaler* Pelagos *ex-*Athenic *in
the breakers' yard at Hamburg in
1962.*

Steamship *Corinthic*
White Star Line, Liverpool

Builders: Harland & Wolff,
Belfast
Yard no: 343
12,231 GRT; 157.1 × 19.3 m /
516 × 63.3 ft; IV exp eng, H & W;
Twin screw; 5,000 IHP; 14 kn;
Passengers: 121 1st class, 117 2nd
class, 450 3rd class.

1902 Apr 10: Launched.
Jul 14: Delivered.
Nov 20: Maiden voyage,
London–Wellington.
1923 Feb: The *Corinthic* rescued
the crew of the American
schooner *Marguerite Ryan*.
1931 Dec 16: Sold for
breaking-up to Hughes, Bolckow
& Co, Blyth.
1932 At Blyth. Later broken-up
at Wallsend.

Steamship *Ionic*
White Star Line, London

Builders: Harland & Wolff,
Belfast
Yard no: 346
12,232 GRT; 157.1 × 19.3 m /
516 × 63.3 ft; IV exp eng, H & W;
Twin screw; 5,000 IHP; 14 kn;
Passengers: 121 1st class, 117 2nd
class, 450 3rd class.

1902 May 22: Launched.
Dec 15: Delivered.
1903 Jan 16: Maiden voyage,
London–Wellington.
1927 The *Ionic* rescued the crew
of the French sailing ship *Daisy*.
1929 Reconstruction of
passenger accommodation; cabin
and third class.
1932 Passenger accommodation
for tourist class only.
1934 Sold to Shaw, Savill &
Albion after merger of White Star
and Cunard Lines. Continued in
New Zealand service.
1937 Jan: Last voyage from
Liverpool to Osaka for
breaking-up.

11 *The* Corinthic *was broken up in 1932.*
12 *The* Ionic *was used in the New Zealand service until 1937.*

The B-Class of the Hamburg-America Line

Steamship *Brasilia*
Hamburg-America Line,
Hamburg

1900 *Norseman*

Builders: Harland & Wolff,
Belfast
Yard no: 318
10,336 GRT; 157.1 × 18.9 m /
516 × 62.0 ft; IV exp eng, H & W;
Twin screw; 4,100 IHP; 12, max
12,5 kn; Passengers: 300 2nd
class, 2,400 steerage; Crew; 150.

1897 Nov 27: Launched.
1898 Mar 21: Completed.
Maiden-voyage Belfast–New
York.
May 4: First voyage
Hamburg–Baltimore.
1900 Feb 12: Sold to Harland &
Wolff, Belfast. Taken over by
Dominion Line, Liverpool.
Renamed *Norseman*. 9,546 GRT.
North Atlantic cargo service.
Accommodation for steerage
passengers.
1910 Jun: First voyage
London–Sydney.
1916 Jan 22: Torpedoed by
German submarine *U 39* in Gulf
of Salonica. Towed to Mudros
and beached. Sold as total loss to
Societa Italiana di Salvataggi e
Nav for breaking-up.
1920 Broken up.

1/2 *After scarcely a year in service,
the* Brasilia *was sold by the
Hamburg-America Line. The ship
was re-constructed by Harland &
Wolff and entered service as the*
Norseman (2) *of the Dominion Line.*

Brasilia.

S.S. "NORSEMAN"

Steamship *Bulgaria*
Hamburg-America Line,
Hamburg

1913 *Canada*; 1913 *Bulgaria*;
1917 *Hercules*; 1919 *Philippines*

Builders: Blohm & Voss,
Hamburg
Yard no: 125
10,237 GRT; 157.4 × 18.9 m /
517 × 62.0 ft; IV exp eng, B & V;
Twin screw; 4,100 IHP; 12, max
12.5 kn; Passengers: 300 2nd
class, 2,400 steerage; Crew: 150.

1898 Feb 5: Launched.
Apr 4: Completed.
Apr 10: Maiden voyage,
Hamburg–New York. Also later
used for service to other US
ports.
1899 Feb 1: Ran into a hurricane
on homeward voyage from New
York. Water came in through
broken hatches. The rudder
smashed. The ship listed badly so
could not be steered using the
propellers. One sailor was swept
overboard.
Feb 2: The *Bulgaria* fired her
distress rockets. 109 injured
horses in the forepart of the ship
had to be killed.
Feb 3: The British steamers
Weehawken, *Vittoria* and
Koordistan came to the rescue,
and took off the passengers after
many hours' work. A child was
killed.
Feb 4: Despite an extensive
search, the three ships lost
contact with the
Hamburg-America steamer. The
Weehawken took the rescued
passengers to Punta Delgade and
reported the *Bulgaria* as sunk.
Feb 9: A short lull in the weather
enabled the crew of the *Bulgaria*

to throw overboard the rotting
horse carcasses.
Feb 10: Renewed storm with
hurricane-force winds.
Feb 14: The British steamer
Antillan came in sight. Five
attempts at towing failed, but
despite the storm she still wanted
to send a boat. The *Bulgaria*
declined the offer with thanks.
Feb 21: Success in constructing
an emergency rudder.
Feb 24: The *Bulgaria* anchored
off Punta Delgada. The crew's
achievement received world-wide
recognition.
1906 After reconstruction by
Blohm & Voss, 11,494 GRT.
1913 Apr 1: Pro-forma sale,
without payment, to Unione
Austriaca di Nav in Trieste
because of rate war with
Canadian Pacific Railway Co.
Renamed *Canada*.
Mediterranean–Canada service.
Back to Hamburg-America as the
Bulgaria.
1914 Aug: Interned in Baltimore.
1917 Apr 6: Seized. Became US
Army transport *Hercules*.
1919 Taken over by US Shipping
Board. Renamed *Philippines*.
1920 Laid up.
1924 Broken up in New York.

Steamship *Batavia*
Hamburg-America Line,
Hamburg
Builders: Blohm & Voss,
Hamburg

1913 *Polonia*;
1913 *Batavia*

Yard no: 132
10,178 GRT; 157.4 × 18.9 m /
517 × 62.0 ft; IV exp eng, B & V;
Twin screw; 4,100 IHP; 12, max
12.5 kn; Passengers: 300 2nd
class, 2,400 steerage; Crew: 150.

1899 Mar 11: Launched.
May 25: Completed.
May 30: Maiden voyage
Hamburg–Baltimore. North
Atlantic service to US ports.
1906 Reconstructed by Blohm &
Voss. 11,464 GRT.
1909 Jun 11: The *Batavia* took
aboard 300 passengers from the
Cunard steamer *Slavonia*, which
had run aground off the Azores
the previous day.
1913 Pro-forma sale, without
payment, to Unione Austriaca di
Nav in Trieste because of rate
war with the Canadian Pacific
Railway Co. Renamed *Polonia*.
Mediterranean–Canada service.
Returned to Hamburg-America
as the *Batavia*.
1917 Naval service as transport
Batavia 7. Took part in
operations against the then
Russian-held island of Oesel in
the Eastern Baltic.
Oct 15: Taken out of naval
service.
1919 Dec 30: Handed over to
French Government.
1924 Broken up.

3 *The* Bulgaria *whose storm torn voyage in 1899 made headlines.*
4 *The* Batavia *after her 1906 reconstruction during which, among other alterations, a deck-house was built around the foot of the foremast.*

Steamship *Belgravia*
Hamburg-America Line,
Hamburg

1905 *Riga*; 1919 *Transbalt*

Builders: Blohm & Voss,
Hamburg
Yard no: 133
10,155 GRT; 157.3 × 18.9 m /
516 × 62.0 ft; IV exp eng, B & V;
Twin screw; 4,100 IHP; 12, max
12.5 kn; Passengers: 300 2nd
class, 2,400 steerage; Crew: 150.

1899 May 11: Launched.
Jul 25: Completed.
Aug 16: Maiden voyage
Hamburg–Baltimore. North
Atlantic service, occasionally
from Mediterranean ports.
1900 Remeasured: 10,982 GRT.
1905 Reconstructed by Blohm &
Voss: 11,397 GRT.
May 31: To Russian Navy;
renamed *Riga*.
1906 Taken over by Black and
Asow Sea SS Co, Odessa.
1919 Renamed *Transbalt* on
take-over by state shipping line
Sovtorgflot.
1920 Hospital ship until 1923.
1945 Jun 13: The *Transbalt* was
mistaken for a Japanese ship by
the US submarine *Spadefish* in
the La Pérouse Channel and
torpedoed.

Steamship *Belgia*
Hamburg-America Line,
Hamburg

1899 *Michigan*; 1900 *Irishman*

Builders: Harland & Wolff,
Belfast
Yard no: 327
11,585 GRT; 157.1 × 18.9 m /
516 × 62.0 ft; IV exp eng, H & W;
Twin screw; 4,100 IHP; 12, max
12.5 kn; Passengers: 300 2nd
class, 2,400 steerage; Crew: 150.

1899 Oct 5: Launched. Intended
for Hamburg–New York service.
Sold before completion to
Atlantic Transport Line, London.
Renamed *Michigan*.
Dec: Trials as cargo ship with
accommodation for steerage
passengers. 9,501 GRT.
1900 Sold to Dominion Line,
Liverpool. Renamed *Irishman*.
1921 Sold to F. Leyland & Co,
Liverpool.
1924 To Holland for breaking-up.
1925 Broken up.

5

5/6/7 *After being sold to the Russians
the* Belgravia *sailed at first under the
name* Riga *and then, after 1920, as
the* Transbalt.
8 *The* Irishman, *of the Dominion
Line, was launched in 1899 as the*
Belgia *for Hamburg-America Line.
As the Baltimore service, for which
Hamburg-America Line had
originally intended to have five B
ships, did not come up to
expectations, the* Belgia *was sold and
then completed as a four masted
vessel.*

6

Учебное судно "Рига". 1906 годъ.

7

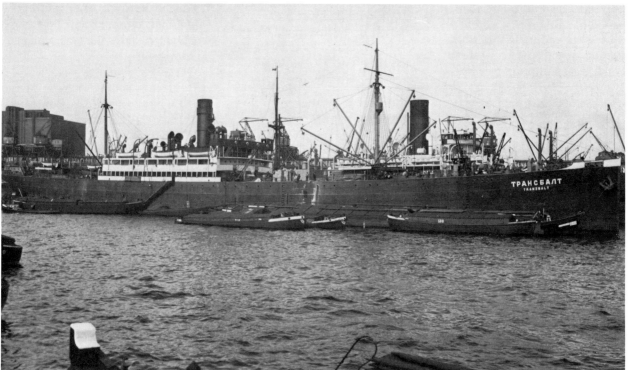

8

German Express Steamers

Steamship *Kaiser Wilhelm der Grosse*
North German Lloyd, Bremen

Builders: 'Vulcan', Stettin
Yard no: 234
14,349 GRT; 199.5 × 20.1 m /
655 × 66.0 ft; III exp eng,
Vulcan; Twin screw; 31,000 IHP;
22, max 23 kn; Passengers: 558
1st class, 338 2nd class, 1,074
steerage; Crew: 488.

1897 May 4: Launched.
Sep 9: Completed – the world's
largest ship until 1899.
Sep 19: Maiden voyage
Bremerhaven–New York.
Nov: *Kaiser Wilhelm der Grosse*
was the first German ship to
succeed in capturing the 'Blue
Riband' with 22.35 kn between
Sandy Hook and the Needles.
1906 Nov 21: Rammed off
Cherbourg by the British steamer
Orinoco and badly damaged. 5
passengers killed.
1913 Only 3rd class and steerage
passengers. 13,952 GRT.
1914 Aug 2: Taken over as
auxiliary cruiser by the German
Navy.
Aug 4: Joined the war against
commerce in the North Atlantic.
Sank three ships with a total
tonnage of 10,500 GRT. The
British passenger ships *Galician*
(6,575 GRT) and *Arlanza* (15,044
GRT) were stopped, but allowed
to proceed as they were carrying
hundreds of passengers.
Aug 26: While bunkering off Rio
del Oro, Spanish West Africa, the
auxiliary cruiser was surprised by
the British cruiser *Highflyer*,
which demanded her surrender.
The German captain refused,
whereupon *Highflyer* opened fire.

After a duel of 90 minutes, the
scarcely damaged
auxiliary-cruiser ran out of
ammunition. The captain gave the
order to abandon the ship, which
was then scuttled with explosive
charges.

Steamship *Kaiser Friedrich*
North German Lloyd, Bremen

1912 Burdigala

Builders: Schichau, Danzig
Yard no: 587
12,481 GRT; 182.9 × 19.4 m /
600 × 63.9 ft; IV exp eng,
Schichau; Twin screw; 28,000
IHP; 19, max 20 kn; Passengers:
400 1st class, 250 2nd class, 700
steerage; Crew: 420.

1897 Oct 5: Launched.
1898 May 12: Completed.
Instead of the required 22 kn, the
ship could scarcely manage 20 kn.
NGL refused to accept her. The
shipyard guaranteed redress, on
the strength of which the ship was
put into service provisionally.
Jun 7: Maiden voyage
Bremerhaven–New York. Sent
back to shipyard after return, as
the top speed was well under 20
kn.
Sep 4: Trials after three months'
reconstruction. Slight
improvement. Three voyages to
New York for NGL, during
which the ship did not exceed 20
kn. Back to shipyard again.
1899 After further
reconstruction, including the
lengthening of each funnel by 14½
ft the *Kaiser Freidrich* was taken
back on trial by NGL, but could

manage only 20 kn.
Jun: The 'Lloyd' finally returned
the ship to Schichau. The affair
became an internationally
observed scandal, which ended
with the defeat in court of the
shipyard.
Oct 1: First voyage in
Hamburg–New York service for
Hamburg-America, who had
chartered the ship on trial.
1900 Oct: After ten round-trips
the Hamburg-America Line
returned the ship to Schichau.
She was laid up in Hamburg.
1912 May 1: The newly formed
Cie Sudatlantique in Bordeaux
bought the ship. After refitting
and installation of new boilers by
Blohm & Voss she was renamed
Burdigala.
Oct 5: First voyage
Bordeaux–South America.
1913 Nov: Laid up in Bordeaux.
1915 Mar: In service as armed
transport for the French Navy.
1916 Nov 14: Ran into mines laid
in the Aegean between Mykonos
and Tenos by U 73, and sank.

1 Kaiser Wilhelm der Grosse *opened
the 'German Decade' in the North
Atlantic in 1897. The steamer won the
'Blue Riband' for Germany for the
first time. German four-funnelled
steamers defended this trophy until
1907.*
2/3 *The* Kaiser Friedrich *was laid up
in Hamburg for 12 years. The Cie
Sudatlantique bought the ship in 1912
and put her into service as the*
Burdigala.

1

2

3

Steamship *Deutschland*
Hamburg-America Line,
Hamburg

1911 *Victoria Luise*; 1921 *Hansa*

Builders: 'Vulcan', Stettin
Yard no: 244
16,502 GRT; 208.5 × 20.4 m /
684 × 67.3 ft; IV exp eng,
Vulcan; Twin screw; 37,800 IHP;
22.5, max 23.5 kn; Passengers:
450 1st class, 300 2nd Class, 300
3rd class. 1,000 berths also
available as steerage when
required; Crew: 536.

1900 Jan 10: Launched.
Jun 25: Completed.
Jul 4: Maiden voyage
Hamburg–New York. The
Deutschland won the 'Blue
Riband' at the first attempt with
an average speed of 22.42 kn
between Eddystone and Sandy
Hook. (22.46 on the return
voyage). In July, 1901, she
improved her record with 23.06
kn westward and 23.51 eastward.
1902 Apr 22: The express
steamer lost her rudder and stern

post in the Atlantic. Repaired by
Blohm & Voss. At the same time,
costly alterations were made to
the engines. Not in service again
until October. The sought-after
improvements in the ship's sailing
qualities were not attained, for the
noisiness of the engines and the
heavy vibration at high speeds
(the cause of the accident on Apr
22) remained unaltered.
1910 Oct: Sent to the 'Vulcan'
shipyard at Stettin, remaining
there until September 1911. Fitted
out as a luxury liner for cruising.
1911 Sep 23: First voyage under
her new name of *Victoria Luise*.
16,703 GRT. 487 1st class
passengers. The rebuilt engines
gave 15,000 IHP with 17.5 knots.
1914 Aug 3: Fitted out as
auxiliary cruiser. Did not enter
service as the boilers were no
longer suitable for high
performance.
1919 The Allies waived their
demand for the surrender of the
ship because of her bad condition.
She thus remained as the only
large steamer under the German

flag.
1920 General overhaul and refit
at the Vulcan shipyard in
Hamburg. The work, delayed by
fires on Oct 13, 1920, and Nov 26,
1920, lasted until Oct, 1921.
1921 Oct 27: First voyage as the
Hansa in Hamburg–New York
service, with accommodation for
36 1st class passengers and 1,350
3rd class. 16,333 GRT.
1922 Reconstruction of
passenger accommodation. 200
cabin class, 664 3rd class. 16,376
GRT.
1924 Hamburg–Canada Service.
Oct: Laid up.
1925 May 15: Sold for
breaking-up.
May 28: Handed over to the
Vulcan shipyard at Hamburg.
Broken up.

4 *The* Deutschland *was the only
Hamburg-America record breaker,
holding the 'Blue Riband' for six
years.*
5 *Victoria Luise, ex-*Deutschland,
*after fitting-out as a cruise liner in
1911.*
6 *In 1920/21 the ship was again
thoroughly refitted; as the* Hansa *she
had only two funnels.*

4

5

6

Steamship *Kronprinz Wilhelm*
North German Lloyd, Bremen

1917 Von Steuben

Builders: 'Vulcan', Stettin
Yard no: 249
14,908 GRT; 202.2 × 20.2 m /
664 × 66.3 ft; IV exp eng,
Vulcan; Twin screw; 36,000 IHP;
22.5, max 23.5 kn; Passengers:
367 1st class, 340 2nd class, 1,054
steerage; Crew: 527.

1901 Mar 30: Launched.
Aug 25: Completed.
Sep 17: Maiden voyage
Bremerhaven–New York.
1914 Aug 3: *Kronprinz Wilhelm*
left New York. Orders: to meet
the cruiser *Karlsruhe* at sea
which would fit her out as an
auxiliary cruiser.
Aug 6: In service as auxiliary
cruiser. In the war against
commerce in the Atlantic she
sank 15 ships of a total of 60,500
GRT.
1915 Apr 10: Sailed into
Newport News. Provisions
exhausted and in serious need of
repairs, she had been forced to
abandon the war in the Atlantic.
Interned on Apr 26.

1917 Apr 6: Seized. Renamed
Von Steuben, US Navy Transport.
1919 Laid up. Handed over to
US Shipping Board.
1920 The New York firm of F.
Eggena chartered the ship with
the intention of sending her on a
world voyage as a floating
exhibition of American goods.
She was to be renamed *United
States*. However, the plan fell
through.
1923 Sold for breaking-up to the
Boston Iron & Steel Metal Co.

7/8 NGL express steamer Kronprinz
Wilhelm *entered service as an
auxiliary cruiser in 1914. In the upper
photo she is pictured after her arrival
in Newport News.*

Steamship *Kaiser Wilhelm II*
North German Lloyd, Bremen

1917 *Agamemnon*;
1929 *Monticello*

Builders: 'Vulcan', Stettin
Yard no: 250
19,361 GRT; 215.3 × 21.9 m /
707 × 72.3 ft; IV exp eng,
Vulcan; Twin screw; 44,500 IHP;
23, max 23.6 kn; Passengers: 775
1st class, 343 2nd class, 770
steerage; Crew: 600.

1902 Aug 12: Launched.
1903 Mar 30: Completed.
Apr 14: Maiden voyage
Bremerhaven–New York.
1906 Jun: *Kaiser Wilhelm II*
broke the *Deutschland's* record
between Sandy Hook and
Eddystone, and wrested the 'Blue
Riband' with a speed of 23.58 kn.
1914 Aug: Interned in New
York.
1917 Apr 6: Seized. Renamed
Agamemnon, US Navy
transport.
1919 Laid up. Handed over to
US Shipping Board. Plans for
purchase and charter by US Mail
Lines and later by United States
Lines not realised.
1929 Renamed *Monticello.* As
reserve ship laid up once more in
Norfolk Navy Yard, and later on
the Patuxent River.
1940 Broken up by the Boston
Iron and Metal Co. Previous to
this, the ship had been offered to
the British Government, who,
however, had declined to take
over the old ship.

9 *North German Lloyd express
steamer* Kaiser Wilhelm II *in New
York.*

9

Steamship *Kronprinzessin Cecilie*
North German Lloyd, Bremen

1917 *Mount Vernon*

Builders: 'Vulcan', Stettin
Yard no: 267
19,360 GRT; 215.3 × 21.9 m /
707 × 72.2 ft; IV exp eng,
Vulcan; Twin screw; 45,000 IHP;
23, max 23.6 kn; Passengers: 742 1st
class, 326 2nd class, 740 steerage;
Crew: 602.

1906 Dec 1: Launched.
1907 Jul 28: Completed.
Aug 6: Maiden voyage
Bremerhaven–New York.
1914 Jul 29: During voyage to
Europe news was received of the
imminent outbreak of war. The
ship was carrying gold bars worth
40 million marks. To avoid the
risk of capture she returned to the
USA, was interned in Bar
Harbour and later in Boston.
1917 Apr 6: Seized by US Navy;
transport *Mount Vernon*.
1918 Sep 5: Torpedoed in boiler
room 200 nautical miles off Brest.
36 dead.
1919 Laid up.
1920 Handed over to US Shipping
Board. Plans for passenger service
with US Mail Lines and United
States Lines; also for her to be
rebuilt as a motor vessel. Neither
project realised.
1924 Laid up in Chesapeake Bay
with sister-ship *Agamemnon,*
ex-*Kaiser Wilhelm II.*
1940 Offered for sale to British
Government. Following their
refusal, she was sent for
breaking-up to the Boston Iron
and Metal Co in Baltimore.

10 *The* Kronprinzessin Cecilie *had
the largest steam reciprocating
machinery ever built into a ship.*
11 *US Navy transport* Mount
Vernon.

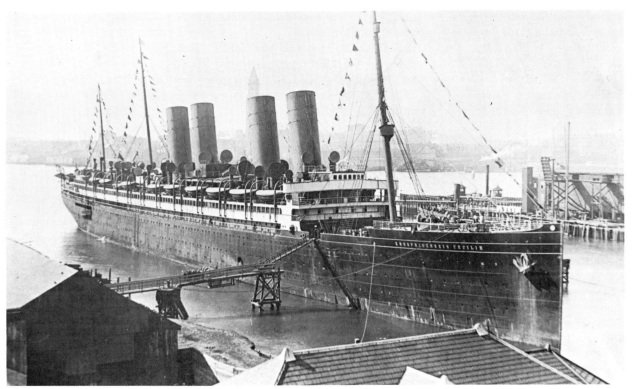

Steamship *Statendam*
Holland-America Line,
Rotterdam

1911 *Scotian*; 1922 *Marglen*

Builders: Harland & Wolff,
Belfast
Yard no: 320
10,491 GRT; 162.8 × 18.2 m /
534 × 59.8 ft; III exp eng, H & W;
Twin screw; 7,000 IHP; 15 kn;
Passengers: 200 1st class, 175
2nd class, 1,000 steerage; Crew:
220.

1898 May 7: Launched.
Aug: Completed.
Aug 24: Maiden voyage
Rotterdam–New York.
1911 Mar 23: Sold to Allan Line,
Glasgow. Renamed *Scotian*;
10,322 GRT. Route: British
ports–Montreal.
1914 Troop transport.
1915 Oct 1: The Allan Line was
taken over by Canadian Pacific.
1918 Overhaul and refit until
1919. New passenger
accommodation became: 304
cabin class, 542 3rd class; 10,417
GRT. Re-entered Montreal

service. Between 1919 and 1922
sailed from Antwerp.
1922 Nov 16: Renamed *Marglen*.
1925 Apr 11: Laid up at
Southampton.
1926 Dec 30: Sold for breaking
up to D. L. Pittaluga, Genoa.
1927 Jan 10: Sailed from
Southampton for Genoa.

Steamship *Potsdam*
Holland-America Line,
Rotterdam

1915 *Stockholm*; 1928 *Solglimt*;
1941 *Sonderburg*

Builders: Blohm & Voss,
Hamburg
Yard no: 139
12,606 GRT; 174.0 × 18.9 m /
571 × 62.2 ft; III exp eng, B & V;
Twin screw; 7,600 IHP; 15 kn;
Passengers: 282 1st class, 210 2nd
class, 1,800 steerage; Crew: 248.

1899 Dec 15: Launched.
1900 May 5: Delivered.
May 17: Maiden voyage
Rotterdam–New York.

1901 Funnel lengthened by 23 ft
to improve furnace draught.
1915 Sep: Sold to Rederie
Sverige Nordamerika, (1925
Swedish-American Line).
Renamed *Stockholm*.
Dec 11: First voyage
Gothenburg–New York.
1922 Converted for oil firing by
Götaverken. Funnel shortened
this time. 15.5 kn. 12,835 GRT.
1928 Nov: Sold to
Hvalfangstakjeselskapet Atlas
(C. Nielsen & Co) Larvik.
Rebuilt as whaling mother-ship by
Götaverken. Renamed *Solglimt*.
12,279 GRT. 11 kn.
1929 Sep 12: In service as
whaler.
1930 Sold to A/S Odde, (A/S
Thor Dahl) Sandefjord.
1941 Jan 14: Captured by the
German auxiliary cruiser *Pinguin*
in the Antarctic, and taken to
Bordeaux as a prize. Taken over
by the Erste Deutsche
Walfanggesellschaft under the
German flag and renamed
Sonderburg.
1944 Jun 15: Scuttled in
Cherbourg.
1947 Jan: Raised. Broken up in
Great Britain.

1

1 *The* Statendam, *the first Dutch
10,000 tonner.*
2/3 *The steamer* Potsdam *on trials
after the lengthening of her funnel
which earned for her the nickname
'Funneldam'.*

Steamship *Rijndam*
Holland-America Line,
Rotterdam

Builders: Harland & Wolff,
Belfast
Yard no: 336
12,527 GRT; 175.3 × 19.0 m /
575 × 62.3 ft; III exp eng, H & W;
Twin screw; 7,500 IHP; 15 kn;
Passengers: 286 1st class, 196
2nd class, 1,800 steerage; Crew:
250.

1901 May 18: Launched.
Oct: Delivered.
Oct 10: Maiden voyage
Rotterdam–New York.
1917 Laid up in New York.
1918 In service as US Navy
transport.
1919 On Rotterdam–New York
route again.
1929 Jan: Broken up at
Hendrik-Ido-Ambacht.

Steamship *Noordam*
Holland-America Line,
Rotterdam

1922 *Kungsholm*; 1924 *Noordam*

Builders: Harland & Wolff,
Belfast
Yard no: 338
12,531 GRT; 175.3 × 19.0 m /
575 × 62.3 ft; III exp eng, H & W;
Twin screw; 7,500 IHP; 15 kn;
Passengers: 286 1st class, 192
2nd class, 1,800 steerage; Crew:
250.

1901 Sep 8: Launched.
1902 Mar: Completed.
May 1: Maiden voyage
Rotterdam–New York.
1917 Aug: Laid up after hitting a
mine.
1919 Mar: Rotterdam–New York
service again.
1922 Mar: Chartered to Reederie
Sverige Nordamerika, renamed
Kungsholm. Gothenburg–New
York service.
1924 Dec: Returned to
Holland-America Line as the

Noordam.
1927 Laid up.
1928 May: To be broken-up by
F. Rijsdijk,
Hendrik-Ido-Ambacht.

4 *The* Stockholm, *ex-*Potsdam, *was
the first ship of the
Swedish-American Line.*
5/6 Rijndam *(5) and* Noordam *(6)
were the Belfast-built sister-ships to
the* Potsdam.

4

5

6

Eight Newly-built British Ships

Steamship *New England*
Dominion Line, Liverpool

1903 *Romanic*;
1912 *Scandinavian*

Builders: Harland & Wolff,
Belfast
Yard no: 315
11,394 GRT; 172.5 × 18.1 m /
566 × 59.3 ft; III exp eng, H & W;
Twin screw; 8,700 IHP; 16 kn;
Passengers: 200 1st class, 200
2nd class, 800 steerage.

1898 Apr 7: Launched.
Jun: Completed.
Jun 30: Maiden voyage
Liverpool–Boston.
1903 Nov: To White Star Line,
Liverpool. Renamed *Romanic*.
Nov 19: First voyage
Liverpool–Boston. From
December Mediterranean–USA.
1912 Jan: To Allan Line,
Glasgow. Renamed
Scandinavian,
Glasgow–Montreal service.
1915 Oct 1: The Allan Line taken
over by Canadian Pacific.

Liverpool–Canada. From 1920,
Antwerp–Canada.
1922 Jul: Laid up.
1923 Jul 9: Sold for breaking-up
to F. Rijsdijk, Rotterdam.
Jul 16: Resold to Klasmann &
Lentze, Emden.

Steamship *Commonwealth*
Dominion Line, Liverpool

1903 *Canopic*

Builders: Harland & Wolff,
Belfast
Yard no: 330
11,394 GRT; 181.0 × 18.1 m /
594 × 59.3 ft; III exp eng, H & W;
Twin screw; 8.700 IHP; 16 kn;
Passengers: 275 1st class, 232 2nd
class, 770 steerage.

1900 May 31: Launched.
Sep: Completed.
Oct 4: Maiden voyage
Liverpool–Boston.
1903 To White Star Line,
Liverpool. Renamed *Canopic*.
12,097 GRT.
1904 Jan 14: First voyage
Liverpool–Boston; then
Mediterranean–USA.
1922 Apr 13:
Liverpool–Montreal.
Nov 10: Bremen–New York.
1923 Nov: Hamburg–New York.
1925 Oct: Sold for breaking-up to
T. W. Ward, and scrapped at
Briton Ferry.

3

Steamship *Winifredian*
F. Leyland, Liverpool

Builders: Harland & Wolff,
Belfast
Yard no: 324
10,405 GRT; 173.6 × 18.1 m /
570 × 59.3 ft; III exp eng, H & W;
Single screw; 5,500 IHP; 14 kn;
Passengers: 135 1st class.

1899 Mar 11: Launched.
Jul: Completed.
Jul 22: Maiden voyage
Liverpool–Boston.
1914 Aug: In transport service
for British Government for the
duration of the war.
1919 Liverpool–Boston service
again.
1927 Antwerp–New York.
1928 Mar: Laid up.
1929 Apr: Sold for breaking-up to
D. L. Pittaluga, Genoa.

1

2

4

1 *The* New England *was delivered to
the Dominion Line in 1898.*
2/3 *The Dominion liner*
Commonwealth *(2) which in 1903 was
transferred within the International
Mercantile Marine Co to the White
Star Line to become the* Canopic *(3).*
4 *Harland & Wolff built the
sister-ships* Winifredian *(4) and*
Devonian *for the Leyland Line.*

Steamship *Devonian*
F. Leyland, Liverpool

Builders: Harland & Wolff,
Belfast
Yard no: 331
10,418 GRT; 173.6 × 18.1 m /
570 × 59.3 ft; III exp eng, H & W;
Single screw; 5,500 IHP; 14 kn;
Passengers: 135 1st class.

1900 Jun 28: Launched.
Sep: Completed.
Sep 15: Maiden voyage
Liverpool–Boston.
1917 Aug 21: Torpedoed and
sunk by German submarine U 53
20 nautical miles northeast of
Tory Island. Two dead.

Steamship *Bavarian*
Allan Line, Glasgow

Builders: Denny, Dumbarton
Yard no: 606
10,376 GRT; 158.5 × 18.1 m /
520 × 59.2 ft; III exp eng,
Denny; Twin screw; 8,000 IHP;
16, max 17.95 kn; Passengers: 240
1st class, 220 2nd class, 1,000
steerage.

1899 May 11: Launched.
Aug 18: Delivered.
Aug 24: Maiden voyage
Liverpool–Montreal. After two
round trips the ship was taken
over by the British Government
for use as a Boer War transport.
1902 Oct 9: Liverpool–Montreal
service again.
1905 Nov 3: Stranded on Wye
Rock off Montreal; later broke
into two.
1906 Nov: The wreck towed to
Quebec.
1907 Scrapped there.

Steamship *Tunisian*
Allan Line, Glasgow

1922 Marburn

Builders: Stephen, Glasgow
Yard no: 384
10,576 GRT; 158.5 × 18.1 m /
520 × 59.2 ft; III exp eng,
Stephen; Twin screw; 8,000 IHP;
16, max 16.9 kn; Passengers: 240
1st class, 220 2nd class, 1,000
steerage.

1900 Jan 17: Launched.
Mar 31: Delivered.
Apr 5: Maiden voyage
Liverpool–Halifax.
1914 Sep 16: In service as troop
transport until 1917.
1915 Oct 1: The Allan Line taken
over by Canadian Pacific.
1920 Reconstruction by D. & W.
Henderson, Glasgow. New
boilers, oil-firing. Passenger
accommodation: 310 cabin, 736
3rd class, 10,743 GRT.
1922 Nov 16: Renamed *Marburn*.
1927 Jul 5: Laid up off Southend.
1928 Feb: Antwerp–Canada
service.
May 9: Laid up at Southampton.
Sep 17: For breaking-up by SA
Co-op Ligure Demolitori Navi,
Genoa.

6

5

7

5 *The Leyland liner* Devonian.
6 *The Allan liner* Bavarian *stranded off Montreal in 1905.*
7 *The* Tunisian *sailed from 1922 as the* Marburn *for Canadian Pacific, which had taken over the Allan Line in 1915.*

Steamship *Haverford*
American Line, Liverpool

Builders: Brown, Clydebank
Yard no: 344
11,635 GRT; 167.6 × 18.0 m /
550 × 59.2 ft; III exp eng, Brown;
Twin screw; 5,000 IHP; 14 kn;
Passengers: 150 2nd class, 1,700
steerage.

1901 May 4: Launched.
Aug: Completed.
Sep 4: Maiden voyage
Southampton–New York. After
two round voyages,
Liverpool–Philadelphia service.
1917 Badly damaged by torpedo
attack off the Irish coast. 11 dead.
Under repair for several months.
1921 To White Star Line,
Liverpool.
Apr 1: First voyage,
Liverpool–Philadelphia.
1922 Hamburg–New York
service.
1924 Dec: Sold to Italian
breakers.

Steamship *Merion*
American Line, Liverpool

1914 *Tiger*

Builders: Brown, Clydebank
Yard no: 345
11,621 GRT; 167.6 × 18.0 m /
550 × 59.2 ft; III exp eng, Brown;
Twin screw; 5,000 IHP; 14 kn;
Passengers: 150 2nd class, 1,700
steerage.

1901 Nov 26: Launched. Before
completion to Dominion Line,
Liverpool.
1902 Feb: Completed.
Mar 8: Maiden voyage
Liverpool–Boston.
1903 To American Line,
Liverpool.
Apr: First voyage
Liverpool–Philadelphia.
1914 Taken over by British
Admiralty. Rebuilt as dummy
battle-cruiser. In service as HMS
Tiger.
1915 May 30: Torpedoed and
sunk in the Aegean off Mudros by
German submarine UB 8.

8/9 *The* Haverford *(8) as a White Star Liner, and her sister-ship* Merion *(9) in the colours of the American Line.*

The Oceanic

Steamship *Oceanic*
White Star Line, Liverpool

Builders: Harland & Wolff,
Belfast
Yard no: 317
17,272 GRT; 214.6 × 20.8 m /
704 × 63.8 ft; III exp eng, H & W;
Twin screw; 28,000 IHP; 19,
max 21 kn; Passengers: 410 1st
class, 300 2nd class, 1,000
steerage.

1899 Jan 14: Launched.
Aug 26: Delivered. Largest ship
in the world until 1901.
Sep 6: Maiden voyage
Liverpool–New York.
1901 Sep: The *Oceanic* ran down
the British coaster *Kincora* in fog
off Tuskar. The latter sank
immediately. Seven dead.
1905 A mutiny on board. 33
stokers subsequently convicted.
1907 Jun 19: First voyage
Southampton–New York.
1914 Aug 8: Auxiliary cruiser in
the 10th cruiser squadron.
Sep 8: Stranded in fog off Foula in
the Shetlands.
Sep 11: Declared total loss.
Breaking-up on the spot
completed in 1924.

3

1

2

1-3 *The express steamer* Oceanic *of the White Star Line*.

Rhein and Main

Steamship *Rhein*
North German Lloyd, Bremen

1917 *Susquehanna*

Builders: Blohm & Voss,
Hamburg
Yard no: 137
10,058 GRT; 158.5 × 17.7 m /
520 × 58.1 ft; IV exp eng, B & V;
Twin screw; 5,500 IHP; 14, max
14.5 kn; Passengers: 369 2nd
class, 217 3rd class, 2,865
steerage (until 1901, 369 1st class,
217 2nd class, 2,865 steerage);
Crew: 174.

1899 Sep 20: Launched.
Dec 4: Completed.
Dec 9: Maiden voyage
Bremerhaven–New York. Later
also used for Baltimore and
Australia service.
1914 Aug: Interned in Baltimore.
1917 Apr 6: Seized. US Navy
transport *Susquehanna*.
1919 Laid up by US Shipping
Board.
1920 Aug 4: First voyage under
charter to US Mail Lines on the
New York–Bremen–Danzig
route. 9,959 GRT.
1921 Aug: Chartered to United
States Lines, New York.
1922 A few voyages New
York–Bremen, and then laid up.
1928 Sold for breaking-up in
Japan.

Steamship *Main*
North German Lloyd, Bremen

Builders: Blohm & Voss,
Hamburg
Yard no: 138
10,067 GRT; 158.5 × 17.7 m /
520 × 58.1 ft; IV exp eng, B & V;
Twin screw; 5,500 IHP; 14, max
14.5 kn; Passengers: 369 2nd
class, 217 3rd class, 2,865
steerage (until 1901: 369 1st class,
217 2nd class, 2,865 steerage);
Crew: 174.

1900 Feb 10: Launched.
Apr 22: Completed.
Apr 28: Maiden voyage
Bremen–New York. Then used
on Baltimore service.
Jun 30: Burnt out and sunk in
New York (see *Bremen* page 22).
Jul 27: Raised by Merrit
Wrecking Co.
Oct 13: Sent to Newport News
for repairs.
1901 Oct 15: In service again
after reconstruction by the
Newport News Shipbuilding &
Dry Dock Co.
1914 The *Main* lay in Antwerp
for the duration of the First World
War.
1919 May 21: Surrendered to
Great Britain and managed for the
Shipping Controller by Turner,
Brightman & Co; from 1920 by
Alfred Holt, Liverpool.
1921 Jun 30: Handed over to
French Government.
1925 Broken up.

1

2

1 *The North German Lloyd
steamship* Rhein.
2 *Arrival for the first time of the* Main
at Bremerhaven.

Steamship *La Lorraine*
CGT, Le Havre

1914 *Lorraine II*;
1917 *La Lorraine*

Builders: Penhoët, St Nazaire
11,146 GRT; 176.8 × 18.3 m /
580 × 60.0 ft; III exp eng,
Penhoët; Twin screw; 22,000
IHP; 20, max 22 kn; Passengers:
446 1st class, 116 2nd class, 552
steerage.

1899 Sept 20: Launched.
1900 Jul: Completed.
Aug 11: Maiden voyage Le
Havre–New York.
1914 Taken up as auxiliary
cruiser *Lorraine II* for French
Navy.
1917 Troop transport, name
reverted to *La Lorraine*.
1919 Le Havre–New York
service.

1922 Dec: Sold for breaking-up
to Penhoët, St Nazaire.

Steamship *La Savoie*
CGT, Le Havre

Builders: Penhoët, St Nazaire
11,168 GRT; 176.8 × 18.3 m /
580 × 60.0 ft; III exp eng,
Penhoët; Twin screw; 22,000
IHP; 20, max 22 kn; Passengers:
437 1st class, 118 2nd class, 500
steerage.

1900 Mar 31: Launched.
1901 Aug: Completed.
Aug 31: Maiden voyage Le
Havre–New York.
1914 Auxiliary cruiser in French
Navy; later a troop transport.
1919 Apr: Back to CGT; New
York service again.
1923 Alterations to passenger

accommodation, 430 cabin class,
613 3rd class.
1927 Nov 24: Sailed from Le
Havre for breaking-up at
Dunkirk.

Steamship *La Provence*
CGT, Le Havre

1914 *Provence II*

Builders: Penhoët, St Nazaire
Yard no: 44
13,753 GRT; 191.0 × 19.8 m /
627 × 65.0 ft; III exp eng,
Penhoët; Twin screw; 31,000
IHP; 21, max 22.7 kn;
Passengers: 422 1st class, 132 2nd
class, 808 steerage.

1905 Mar 21: Launched.
1906 Apr: Completed.
Apr 21: Maiden voyage Le
Havre–New York.

1914 In service as French Navy's auxiliary cruiser *Provence II*.
1916 Feb 26: Torpedoed in Mediterranean by German submarine U 35. *Provence II* had troops on board as well as her crew. 930 dead.

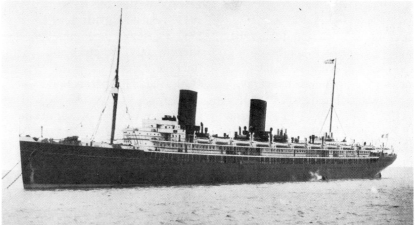

1/2 *The Cie Générale Transatlantique brought their express fleet up to international standard with the sister-ships* La Lorraine *(1) and* La Savoie *(2).*
3 La Provence *was a development of the two earlier express steamers.*
4 *The auxiliary cruiser* Provence II.

Ivernia and Saxonia

Steamship *Ivernia*
Cunard Line, Liverpool

Builders: C. S. Swan & Hunter,
Newcastle
Yard no: 247
13,799 GRT; 182.9 × 19.7 m /
600 × 64.9 ft; IV exp eng,
Wallsend Slipway; Twin screw;
10,500 IHP; 15, max 16.8 kn;
Passengers: 164 1st class, 200 2nd
class, 1,600 steerage.

1899 Sep 21: Launched.
1900 Mar: Completed.
Apr 14: Maiden voyage
Liverpool–New York. After
three New York round trips she
entered the Liverpool–Boston
service. The *Ivernia's* tonnage
measurement changed several
times; she is noted as 14,058 GRT
in 1902, 14,067 GRT in 1908, and
14,278 GRT in 1913.
1912 Trieste–New York service.
1917 Jan 1: The *Ivernia* was
torpedoed and sunk near Cape
Matapan by the German
submarine *UB 47*. 36 dead.

Steamship *Saxonia*
Cunard Line, Liverpool

Builders: Brown, Clydebank
Yard no: 339
14,281 GRT; 182.9 × 19.5 m /
600 × 64.2 ft; IV exp eng, Brown;
Twin screw; 10,400 IHP; 15, max
16.8 kn; Passengers: 164 1st
class, 200 2nd class, 1,600
steerage.

1899 Dec 16: Launched.
1900 May: Completed.
May 22: Maiden voyage
Liverpool–Boston.
1911 Trieste–Boston service.
1912 Passenger accommodation
altered; only 2nd class and
steerage.
1914 Aug: Troop transport. After
one voyage she was used to house
German prisoners of war on the
Thames.
1915 Mar: Troop transport once
more.
1919 Jan 25: First post-war
voyage, Liverpool–New York.
1920 Refitted at Tilbury. Funnel
shortened by 16 ft. Passengers:
471 cabin class, 978 3rd class.
14,197 GRT.
New York service from London.
Later from Hamburg.
1925 Mar: Sold for breaking-up at
Hendrik Ido Ambacht.

1/2 *In 1900 Cunard Line placed the
steamships* Ivernia *(1) and* Saxonia
(2) on the Liverpool–Boston service.
3 *The* Saxonia *in 1920 after
alterations.*

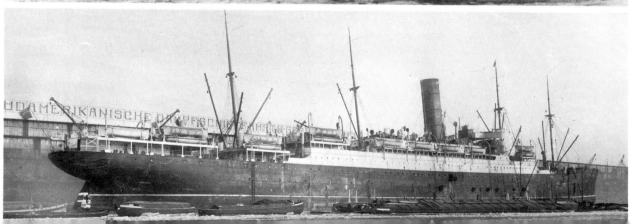

Steamship *Minneapolis*
Atlantic Transport Line, Belfast

Builders: Harland & Wolff,
Belfast
Yard no: 328
13,401 GRT; 187.8 × 19.8 m /
616 × 65.5 ft; IV exp eng, H & W;
Twin screw; 10,000 IHP; 16 kn;
Passengers: 228 1st class.

1899 Nov 18: Launched.
1900 May: Completed.
May 10: Maiden voyage
London–New York.
1915 Troop transport.
1916 Mar 23: The *Minneapolis*
was torpedoed and sunk northeast
of Malta by the German
submarine U 35. 12 dead.

Steamship *Minnehaha*
Atlantic Transport Line, Belfast

Builders: Harland & Wolff,
Belfast
Yard no: 329
13,403 GRT; 187.8 × 19.8 m /
616 × 65.5 ft; IV exp eng, H & W;
Twin screw; 10,000 IHP; 16 kn;
Passengers: 228 1st class.

1900 Mar 1: Launched.
Jul: Completed.
Aug 11: Maiden voyage
London–New York.
Collision in New York harbour
with the tugboat *American*, which
sank with the loss of two of her
crew.
1910 Apr 18: The *Minnehaha* ran
aground off the Scilly Isles. It was
not possible to refloat her until
May 13.
1917 Sep 7: The *Minnehaha* was
torpedoed by the German
submarine U 48 12 nautical miles

off Fastnet, and sank in 4
minutes. 43 dead.

Steamship *Minnetonka*
Atlantic Transport Line, Belfast

Builders: Harland & Wolff,
Belfast
Yard no: 339
13,398 GRT; 187.8 × 19.8 m /
616 × 65.5 ft; IV exp eng, H & W;
Twin screw; 10,000 IHP; 16 kn;
Passengers: 250 1st class.

1901 Dec 12: Launched.
1902 Jul: Completed.
Jul 12: Maiden voyage
London–New York.
1915 Mar: Troop transport.
1918 Jan 31: Torpedoed and sunk
40 nautical miles northwest of
Malta by German submarine
U 64. Four dead.

1

2

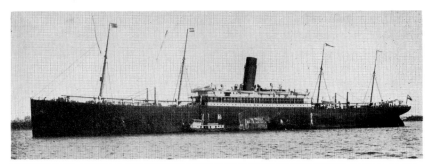

3

4

1/2 *The* Minneapolis *arrives in New York for the first time.*
3/4 *The ATL liner* Minnehaha.
5 *The third ship of the trio in the London–New York service, the* Minnetonka. *All three ships were victims of submarine warfare during the First World War.*

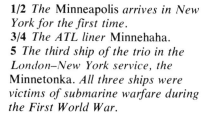

5

Steamship *Vaderland*
Red Star Line, Liverpool

1915 *Southland*

Builders: Brown, Clydebank
Yard no: 341
12,018 GRT; 176.8 × 18.3 m /
580 × 60.2 ft; IV exp eng, Brown;
Twin screw; 10,000 IHP; 15, max
17 kn; Passengers: 342 1st class,
194 2nd class, 626 steerage.

1900 Jul 12: Launched.
Nov 29: Delivered.
Dec 8: Maiden voyage
Antwerp–New York.
1903 Registered in Antwerp.
1914 To White Star Line,
Liverpool.
Sep 3: First voyage New
York–Liverpool.
1915 Renamed *Southland*.
Liverpool–Montreal service, then
troop transport.
1917 Jun 4: The *Southland* was
sunk 140 nautical miles northwest
of Tory Island by two torpedoes
from the German submarine
U 70. Four dead.

Steamship *Zeeland*
Red Star Line, Liverpool

1915 *Northland*; 1920 *Zeeland*;
1927 *Minnesota*

Builders: Brown, Clydebank
Yard no: 342
11,905 GRT; 176.8 × 18.3 m /
580 × 60.2 ft; IV exp eng, Brown;
Twin screw; 10,000 IHP; 15, max
17 kn; Passengers: 342 1st class,
194 2nd class, 626 steerage.

1900 Nov 24: Launched.
1901 Apr 5: Delivered.
Apr 13: Maiden voyage
Antwerp–New York.
1910 First voyage,
Liverpool–Boston, for White Star
Line.
1911 Sep: Red Star Line again,
Antwerp–New York service.
1912 Registered in Antwerp for
the Red Star Line.
1914 Sep: First Liverpool–New
York voyage; later on Canada
service.
1915 Feb: Renamed *Northland*.
Troop transport, civilian service
and voyages for the Shipping
Controller until 1919.
1920 Returned to Red Star Line,
Liverpool, after overhaul and
conversion to oil firing at Belfast
and Antwerp. Renamed *Zeeland*.
Aug 18: First Antwerp–New
York voyage; occasionally also
Hamburg–New York.
1924 Reconstruction of
passenger accommodation to
tourist-class only. 11,667 GRT.
1927 Jan: Sold to Atlantic
Transport Line, Liverpool.
Renamed *Minnesota* after one
voyage London–Shanghai as a
troop transport.
Apr: First London–New York
voyage.

1929 Oct: Sold to T. W. Ward for
breaking-up.
1930 Scrapped at Inverkeithing.

1

2

3

1 *The Red Star Line, which belonged to the International Mercantile Marine Co, had four steamers built for the Antwerp–New York service. The* Vaderland *sailed from 1903 until 1914 under the Belgian flag.*
2/3 *The* Zeeland *also sometimes flew the Belgian flag.*

Steamship *Kroonland*
Red Star Line, New York

Builders: Cramp, Philadelphia
Yard no: 311
12,760 GRT; 182.9 × 18.3 m /
600 × 60.2 ft; III exp eng, Cramp;
Twin screw; 10,700 IHP; 15, max
17 kn; Passengers: 343 1st class,
194 2nd class, 1,000 steerage.

1902 Feb 8: Launched.
May: Trials.
Jun 28: Maiden voyage New
York–Antwerp.
1908 Until 1911 registered in
Antwerp for the Red Star Line.
1913 Oct 9: The *Kroonland*
rescued 90 survivors from the
Volturno fire disaster (see page
26).
1914 Aug: New York–Liverpool
route after outbreak of war.
1916 North Atlantic service for
American Line.
1918 Apr: Taken over by US
Navy as armed transport.
1919 Sep: Released from naval
service. Refitted for passenger
carrying. Passengers: 242 1st
class, 310 2nd class, 876 3rd class.
12,241 GRT.
1920 Apr: Red Star Line again,
New York–Antwerp, sometimes
to Hamburg.
1923 Sold to American Line,
New York.
Jun 21: First voyage New
York–Hamburg.
Oct: Sold to Panama Pacific Line,
New York, New York–San
Francisco service.
1925 New York–Miami service.
1926 Mar: Laid up in New York.
1927 Jan: Sold for breaking-up at
Genoa.

Steamship *Finland*
Red Star Line, New York

Builders: Cramp, Philadelphia
Yard no: 312
12,760 GRT; 182.9 × 18.3 m /
600 × 60.2 ft; III exp eng, Cramp;
Twin screw; 10,700 IHP; 15, max
17 kn; Passengers: 343 1st class,
194 2nd class, 1,000 steerage.

1902 Jun 2: Launched.
Sep: Completed.
Oct 4: Maiden voyage New
York–Antwerp.
1914 Aug: New York–Liverpool
route after outbreak of war; from
1916 under control of the
American Line.
1918 Armed transport for US
Navy.
1919 Returned to Red Star Line;
refitted as passenger ship.
1920 Apr: New York–Antwerp
service again; this was sometimes
extended to Hamburg.
1923 Apr: Sold to American
Line, New York.
May 31: First voyage, New
York–Hamburg.
Nov: Sold to Panama Pacific
Line, New York. New York–San
Francisco service.
1928 Feb: Sold for breaking-up to
Hughes, Bolckow; scrapped at
Blyth.

4-6 *The sister-ships* Kroonland *and*
Finland *were built in the USA and
sailed under the American flag.*

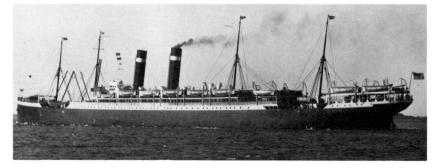

5

6

Pacific Mail Liners

Steamship *Korea*
Pacific Mail SS Co, New York

1916 *Korea Maru*

Builders: Newport News
Shipbuilding & Dry Dock Co
Yard no: 31
11,276 GRT; 174.3 × 19:3 m /
572 × 63.0 ft; IV exp eng from
hull builders; Twin screw; 18,000
IHP; 17, max 20 kn; Passengers:
300 1st class, 60 steerage for
Europeans, 1,200 steerage for
Asiatics; Crew: 236.

1901 Mar 23: Launched.
1902 Mar: Trials.
Jun: Delivered.
Sep 30: Maiden voyage San
Francisco–Hong Kong. Fastest
ship on the Transpacific route.
1915 Aug: Sold to Atlantic
Transport Co of West Virginia,
New York. Placed on New
York–London service.
1916 Jul: Sold to Toyo Kisen
Kaisha, Yokohama. Renamed
Korea Maru. Transpacific service.
11,810 GRT.
1923 Sep 1: Provided assistance
following the great Tokyo
earthquake.
1925 Toyo Kisen Kaisha was
taken over by Nippon Yusen
Kaisha.
1930 Laid up in Kobe.
1934 Sold for breaking-up in
Japan.

Steamship *Siberia*
Pacific Mail SS Co, New York

1916 *Siberia Maru*

Builders: Newport News
Shipbuilding & Dry Dock Co
Yard no: 32
11,284 GRT; 174.3 × 19.3 m /
572 × 63.0 ft; IV exp eng from
hull builders; Twin screw; 18,000
IHP; 17, max 20 kn; Passengers:
300 1st class, 60 steerage for
Europeans, 1,200 steerage for
Asiatics; Crew: 236.

1901 Oct 19: Launched.
1902 Dec: Delivered.
1903 Jan: Maiden voyage San
Francisco–Hong Kong.
1915 Aug: Sold to Atlantic
Transport Co of West Virginia,
New York. New York–London
service.
1916 Jul: Sold to Toyo Kisen
Kaisha, Yokohama. Renamed
Siberia Maru. Transpacific
service. 11,785 GRT.
1925 Toyo Kisen Kaisha was
taken over by Nippon Yusen
Kaisha.
1930 Laid up.
1935 Broken up in Japan.

Steamship *Mongolia*
Pacific Mail SS Co, New York

1929 *President Fillmore*;
1940 *Panamanian*

Builders: New York Shipbuilding
Corp, Camden
Yard no: 5
13,639 GRT; 187.8 × 19.9 m /
616 × 65.3 ft; IV exp eng from
hull builders; Twin screw; 10,000
IHP; 16 kn; Passengers: 350 1st
class, 68 2nd class, 1,400
steerage.

1903 Jul 24: Launched. The ship
had originally been ordered by the
Atlantic Transport Co of West
Virginia, New York for their
North Atlantic service. Intended
name: *Minnelora*.
To Pacific Mail before launching.
1904 Jan 27: Trials.
Feb 20: Delivered. Entered
service on San Francisco–Hong
Kong route.
1915 To Atlantic Transport Co of
West Virginia.
1916 New York–London service.
1918 Armed transport for US
Navy.
1919 New York–Hamburg
service under control of the
American Line.
1923 To Panama Pacific Line,
New York.
1924 Reconstruction and
modernisation in New York.
Passengers: 267 1st class, 1,370
3rd class. 15,442 GRT.
1925 New York–San Francisco
service.
1926 Passengers: 240 1st class,
834 cabin class.

1929 Sold to Dollar Line, San Francisco. Renamed *President Fillmore*. 15,575 GRT. Round the world service.
1931 Laid up in New York.
1938 The Dollar Line was taken over by the US Government and continued as American President Lines.
1940 Sold to Cia Transatlantica Centroamericana, Panama, an enterprise founded by the former Hamburg ship owner Arnold Bernstein, after he had left Germany. Renamed *Panamanian*.
1946 Broken up in Hong Kong.

1/2 The Korea *(1) and the* Siberia *(2) were the fastest Transpacific ships of their time. They were interesting, and for passenger ships rather unusual, in that their port side appearance was different from that of the starboard side.*
The superstructure covering the port side of the main deck was open, but on the starboard side metal plating covered everything up to promenade deck level.
3 *The* Korea Maru *when she belonged to the Toyo Kisen Kaisha.*
4 *Pacific Mail liner* Mongolia. *The sister-ships* Mongolia *and* Manchuria *had long and varied careers which were almost identical for each ship.*

Steamship *Manchuria*
Pacific Mail SS Co, New York

1929 *President Johnson*;
1947 *Santa Cruz*

Builders: New York Shipbuilding
Corp, Camden
Yard no: 6
13,639 GRT; 187.8 × 19.9 m /
616 × 65.3 ft; IV exp eng from
hull builders; Twin screw; 10,000
IHP; 16 kn; Passengers: 350 1st
class, 68 2nd class, 1,300
steerage.

1903 Oct 31: Launching planned,
but the ship stuck half way.
Nov 2: Launched. Originally
ordered by the Atlantic Transport
Co of West Virginia for their
North Atlantic service, to be
named *Minnekahda*. To
Pacific Mail Line before
launching.
1904 Jun 9: Delivered. Entered
Transpacific service, San
Francisco–Hong Kong.
1915 To Atlantic Transport Co of
West Virginia, New York.
1916 New York–London service.
1918 Armed transport in US
Navy.
1919 New York–Hamburg
service for American Line.

1923 To Panama Pacific Line,
New York. New York–San
Francisco service.
1924 Reconstruction and
modernisation. Passengers: 265
1st class, 1,350 3rd class. 15,445
GRT.
1926 Passengers: 240 1st class,
834 cabin class.
1928 Oct: To the Dollar Line,
San Francisco.
1929 Renamed *President
Johnson*. 15,543 GRT. Round the
world service.
1932 Laid up until 1933, and
again from 1936 to 1941.
1938 The Dollar Line was taken
over by the US Government and
continued as American President
Lines.
1941 Transport for US
Government.
1946 Jan: Laid up.
1947 Sold to Tagus Navigation
Co SA Lisbon. Renamed *Santa
Cruz*. 16,111 GRT, Lisbon–La
Plata service.
1948 Registered in Panama for
the Soc Empresas Maritimas SA,
on charter to the 'Italia' Societa
per Azioni di Nav. South
American service from
Mediterranean ports. 15,511 GRT.
1952 Broken up in Savona.

5

5 *The* Mongolia *in 1916 with
American neutrality markings.*
6 *In 1923 the* Manchuria *came under
the flag of the Panama Pacific Line.*
7 Santa Cruz *was the last name of
the old* Manchuria.

White Star's 'Big Four'

Steamship *Celtic*
White Star Line, Liverpool

Builders: Harland & Wolff,
Belfast
Yard no: 335
20,904 GRT; 213.4 × 22.9 m /
700 × 75.3 ft; IV exp eng, H & W;
Twin screw; 14,000 IHP; 16, max
16.5 kn; Passengers: 347 1st class,
160 2nd class, 2,350 steerage.

1901 Apr 4: Launched.
Jul 11: Delivered.
Jul 26: Maiden voyage
Liverpool–New York. Until 1903
the *Celtic* was the largest ship in
the world.
1914 Oct 20: Auxiliary cruiser in
the 10th Cruiser Squadron.
1916 Jan: Troop transport.
1917 Mar: Struck by torpedo in
the Irish Sea. Six dead. Repaired
at Belfast.
1918 Dec 8: First postwar voyage
Liverpool–New York.
1920 Passenger accommodation
altered: 350 1st class, 250 2nd
class, 1,000 3rd class.
1928 Dec 10: The *Celtic* stranded
in a storm at Roches Point by the
entrance into Cobh, Ireland. All
salvage attempts failed. The
wreck was sold to Petersen &
Albeck, Copenhagen, who
completed breaking-up in 1933.

Steamship *Cedric*
White Star Line, Liverpool

Builders: Harland & Wolff,
Belfast
Yard no: 337
21,035 GRT; 213.4 × 22.9 m /
700 × 75.3 ft; IV exp eng, H & W;
Twin screw; 15,000 IHP; 16, max
17 kn; Passengers: 365 1st class,
160 2nd class, 2,350 steerage.

1902 Aug 21: Launched.
1903 Jan 31: Delivered. Until
1904 the largest ship in the world.
Feb 11: Maiden voyage
Liverpool–New York.
1914 Dec 4: Auxiliary cruiser
with the 10th Cruiser Squadron.
1915 Troop and supply transport
until end of war.
1918 Jan 29: Collision off the
Mersey Bar with the Canadian
Pacific steamer *Montreal;* the
latter sank.
Dec 14: First postwar voyage
Liverpool–New York.
1920 Steerage accommodation
rebuilt for 1,000 3rd class
passengers.
1931 Sold for breaking-up to T.
W. Ward.
1932 Jan 11: Last voyage from
Liverpool for breaking-up at
Inverkeithing.

1

2

3

1 *The White Star liner* Celtic *was the first ship in the world to exceed 20,000 GRT.*
2 *The* Celtic *ashore off Cobh.*
3 *The* Cedric *which entered service in 1903. With the four ships of the Celtic-class, the White Star Line had finally moved away from express steamers, and was pinning its future hopes on the large, comfortably fitted out ship with a more economical medium speed.*

Steamship *Baltic*
White Star Line, Liverpool

Builders: Harland & Wolff,
Belfast
Yard no: 352
23,884 GRT; 221.3 × 23.0 m /
726 × 75.5 ft; IV exp eng,. H & W;
Twin screw; 15,000 IHP; 16, max
17 kn; Passengers: 425 1st class,
450 2nd class, 2,000 steerage.

1903 Nov 21: Launched.
1904 Jun 23: Delivered. Largest
ship in the world until 1905.
Jun 29: Maiden voyage
Liverpool–New York.
1909 Jan 23: The *Baltic* took
aboard survivors from the
Republic, which had collided with
the Italian *Florida* in fog near
Nantucket.
1914 Used occasionally as a
troop transport during the First
World War.
1921 Steerage accommodation
altered to take about 1,000 3rd
class passengers.
1924 Reboilered.
1929 Dec 6: Rescue of the crew
of the sinking schooner *Northern
Light.*
1932 Oct: Laid up.
1933 Feb 17: Last voyage
Liverpool–Osaka for
breaking-up.

Steamship *Adriatic*
White Star Line, Liverpool

Builders: Harland & Wolff,
Belfast
Yard no: 358
24,541 GRT; 221.3 × 23.0 m /
726 × 75.6 ft; IV exp eng, H & W;
Twin screw; 17,000 IHP; 17, max
18 kn; Passengers: 425 1st class,
500 2nd class, 1,900 steerage;
Crew: 557.

1906 Sep 20: Launched.
1907 Apr: Completed.
May 8: Maiden voyage,
Liverpool–New York.
Jun 5: First voyage
Southampton–New York.
1911 Aug 24: Again
Liverpool–New York.
1919 Passengers: 400 1st class,
465 2nd class, 1,320 3rd class.
Sep 3: Southampton–New York
service; from May 1922 again
Liverpool–New York.
1922 Aug 11: Five dead and four
injured after explosion in a coal
bunker.
1928 Passengers: 506 cabin class,
560 tourist class, 404 3rd class.
1933 Aug: Laid up in Liverpool.
1934 Feb: Cunard Line and
White Star Line merged to form
the Cunard-White Star Line. The
Adriatic entered service once
more, but was laid up again in
September.
1934 Nov: Sold for breaking-up
in Japan.
1935 Mar 5: Arrived in Osaka.
Scrapped there.

4

4 *The* Baltic *on the stocks at the Harland & Wolff yard.*
5/6 *The* Baltic *(5) and the* Adriatic *(6) entered service in 1904 and 1907 respectively. They were somewhat larger and faster than the first two members of the quartet.*

5

6

Steamship *Oscar II*
Det Forenede D/S, Copenhagen

Builders: Stephen, Glasgow
Yard no: 393
10,012 GRT; 158.0 × 17.8 m /
519 × 58.2 ft; III exp eng,
Stephen; Twin screw; 8,500 IHP;
15, max 16 kn; Passengers: 130
1st class, 140 2nd class, 900
steerage.

1901 Nov 14: Launched.
1902 Feb: Completed. The ship
was measured at 9,970 GRT until
1921.
Mar 12: Maiden voyage
Copenhagen–New York.
1931 Laid up.
1933 Sep: Sold for breaking-up.
1934 Broken up by Hughes,
Bolckow & Co, Blyth.

Steamship *Hellig Olav*
Det Forenede D/S, Copenhagen

Builders: Stephen, Glasgow
Yard no: 399
10,085 GRT; 158.5 × 17.8 m /
520 × 58.2 ft; III exp eng,
Stephen; Twin screw; 8,500 IHP;
15, max 16 kn; Passengers: 130
1st class, 140 2nd class, 900
steerage.

1902 Dec 16: Launched.
1903 Mar 17: Delivered.
Mar 26: Maiden voyage
Copenhagen–New York.
1931 Laid up.
1933 Dec: Sold for breaking-up.
1934 Broken up by Hughes,
Bolckow & Co, Blyth.

Steamship *United States*
Det Forenede D/S, Copenhagen

Builders: Stephen, Glasgow
Yard no: 400
10,095 GRT; 158.5 × 17.8 m /
520 × 58.2 ft; III exp eng,
Stephen; Twin screw; 8,500 IHP;
15, max 16.5 kn; Passengers: 131
1st class, 76 2nd class, 1,306
steerage.

1903 Mar 30: Launched.
Mar 15: Delivered.

Jun 3: Maiden voyage
Copenhagen–New York.
1934 Laid up.
1935 Broken up at Leghorn,
Italy.

1/2 Steamship Oscar II *in
Copenhagen Harbour (1) and with
neutrality markings during the First
World War.*

1

2

3

4

3 *The* Hellig Olav, *which entered service in 1902.*
4 *Steamship* United States *in the 'twenties with the forward section of her boat-deck glass-enclosed. The Forenede D/S had taken over the North Atlantic service of the Thingvalla Line in 1898, and continued it under the new name of Scandinavia-America Line. The out-of-date fleet was replaced by these three ships.*

Steamship *Hanoverian*
Leyland Line, Liverpool

1903 *Mayflower*; 1903 *Cretic*;
1923 *Devonian*

Builders: Hawthorn, Leslie,
Newcastle
Yard no: 381
13,507 GRT; 183.2 × 18.4 m /
601 × 60.3 ft; III exp eng from
hull builders; Twin screw; 8,500
IHP; 15 kn; Passengers: 245 1st
class, 250 2nd class, 1,000
steerage.

1902 Feb 25: Launched.
Jun: Completed.
Jul 19: Maiden voyage
Liverpool–Boston.
1903 Apr: To Dominion Line,
Liverpool. Renamed *Mayflower*.
Apr 9: First voyage
Liverpool–Boston.
Nov: To White Star Line,
Liverpool. Renamed *Cretic*.
Nov 26: First voyage, same
route.
1904 Entered
Mediterranean–USA route.
1915 Troop and supply transport
until 1919.
1919 Mediterranean–USA again,
with accommodation for 300 1st
class, 200 2nd class and 800 3rd
class passengers.
1923 To Leyland Line,
Liverpool; renamed *Devonian*,
Liverpool–Boston service.
1927 Antwerp–New York
service for Red Star Line.
1928 Mar 9: Laid up.
1929 Jan: Sold for breaking-up to
P. & W. McLellan, Bo'ness.

Steamship *Columbus*
Dominion Line, Liverpool

1903 *Republic*

Builders: Harland & Wolff,
Belfast
Yard no: 345
15,378 GRT; 178.3 × 20.6 m /
585 × 67.8 ft; IV exp eng, H & W;
Twin screw; 10,000 IHP; 16 kn;
Passengers: 1st class, 2nd class,
and steerage (exact numbers
unknown).

1903 Feb 26: Launched.
Sep 12: Delivered.
Oct 1: Maiden voyage
Liverpool–Boston.
Dec: To White Star Line,
Liverpool. Renamed *Republic*.
Dec 17: First voyage
Liverpool–Boston.
1909 USA–Mediterranean
service.
Jan 23: On a voyage New York–
Genoa the *Republic* collided in
fog with the Italian steamer
Florida near the Nantucket
lightship. Both ships were badly
damaged, and the *Republic* began
to sink. She had nearly 2,000
people on board. The *Republic*
sent out the first radio distress
message in the history of sea
travel. Several ships set course
for the position of the casualty.
The White Star liner *Baltic* was
able to take aboard the survivors
from the *Republic*. Four people,
however, had been killed in the
collision. Some American
coasters tried to take the *Republic*
in tow, but she sank the following
morning.

1/2 *The Leyland Liner* Hanoverian *(1)*
on her first outward voyage and in (2)
as the White Star Liner Cretic.
3 *The White Star Liner* Republic,
*ex-*Columbus, *sank after a collision in*
fog in 1909.

Steamship *Carpathia*
Cunard Line, Liverpool

Builders: C. S. Swan & Hunter,
Newcastle
Yard no: 274
13,564 GRT; 170.1 × 19.6 m /
558 × 64.5 ft; IV exp eng,
Wallsend Slipway; Twin screw;
9,000 IHP; 15 kn; Passengers: 204
1st class, 1,500 steerage.

1902 Aug 6: Launched.
1903 Aug 22: Trials.
May 5: Maiden voyage
Liverpool–Boston.
1904 Used variously on
Trieste–New York and
Liverpool–New York routes.
1912 Apr 15: The *Carpathia*
picked up the distress signal of the
sinking *Titanic* and sailed at
utmost speed to the stated
position. When she reached the
scene of the disaster in the early
hours of the morning, the *Titanic*
had already sunk. The *Carpathia*
picked up the 700 survivors and
took them to New York.
1918 Jul 17: On a voyage from
Liverpool to the USA the
Carpathia was hit by three
torpedoes from the German
submarine U 55 and sank 170
nautical miles from Bishop's
Rock. Five dead.

Steamship *Ultonia*
Cunard Line, Liverpool

Builders: C. S. Swan & Hunter,
Newcastle
Yard no: 228
10,402 GRT; 156.4 × 17.5 m /
513 × 57.4 ft; III exp eng,
Furness, Westgarth; Twin screw;
4,500 IHP; 13 kn; Passengers:
Steerage only.

1898 Jun 4: Launched.
Oct: Completed.
Oct 28: Maiden voyage
Newcastle–Boston. Afterwards
Liverpool–Boston service.
1899 Measured as 8,845 GRT;
shelter decker until 1903.
1904 Entered Trieste–New York
service.
1912 A few London–Montreal
voyages.
1917 Jun 27: The *Ultonia* was
torpedoed and sunk 190 nautical
miles southwest of Fastnet by the
German submarine U 53. One
dead.

Steamship *Slavonia*
Cunard Line, Liverpool

Ex-*Yamuna*

Builders: Laing, Sunderland
Yard no: 600
10,606 GRT; 160.3 × 18.1 m /
526 × 59.5 ft; III exp eng,
Wallsend Slipway; Twin screw;
5,000 IHP; 13 kn; Passengers: 40
1st class, 800 steerage.

1902 Nov 15: Launched as the
Yamuna for British India Line.
1903 Jun 20: Completed. 8,831
GRT.
1904 Bought by Cunard Line.
Refitted for North Atlantic
service. Renamed *Slavonia*.
Mar 17: First voyage
Sunderland–Trieste, then
Trieste–New York service.
1909 Jun 10: Ashore near Flores,
in the Azores, on a voyage from
New York to Trieste. The
passengers were taken off by the
German steamers *Prinzess Irene*
and *Batavia,* which had been
called to the scene. The
Slavonia had to be written off as a
total loss.

4 *The Cunarder* Carpathia *became
world-famous through her rescue of
survivors from the* Titanic.

4

5

6

7

5 *The* Ultonia *sailed until 1903 mainly as a livestock carrier before she entered Cunard Line's Mediterranean–USA service.*
6 *The Cunard steamer* Slavonia *stranded off the Azores.*
7 *The* Yamuna, *which was rebuilt to become the* Slavonia.

Steamship *Arabic*
White Star Line, Liverpool

Builders: Harland & Wolff,
Belfast
Yard no: 340
15,801 GRT; 187.8 × 19.8 m /
616 × 65.5 ft; IV exp eng, H & W;
Twin screw; 10,000 IHP; 16 kn;
Passengers: 1st and 2nd class and
steerage (exact numbers not
known).

1902 Dec 18: Launched.
Originally ordered by the Atlantic
Transport Line as a sister-ship to
the *Minnetonka* for the
London–New York service,
under name of *Minnewaska*.
To White Star Line before
launching.
1903 Jun: Delivered.

Jun 26: Maiden voyage
Liverpool–New York.
1905 Liverpool–Boston route
until 1907, then New York service
again.
1911 Boston service again, and
then Liverpool–New York from
December, 1914.
1915 Aug 19: The *Arabic* was
torpedoed and sunk off the Old
Head of Kinsale, Southern
Ireland, by the German submarine
U 24. 44 dead.

8/9 *White Star Line's* Arabic,
originally ordered by ATL.

Steamship *Majestic*
White Star Line, Liverpool

Builders: Harland & Wolff,
Belfast
Yard no: 209
10,147 GRT; 177.4 × 17.6 m /
582 × 57.8 ft; III exp eng, H & W;
Twin screw; 17,500 IHP; 19, max
20 kn; Passengers: 300 1st class,
170 2nd class, 850 3rd class.

1889 Jun 29: Launched.
1890 Mar 22: Delivered. 9,965
GRT.
Apr 2: Maiden voyage
Liverpool–New York.
1891 Jul: The *Majestic* gained the
'Blue Riband' for the westward
run with a speed of 20.1 kn.
However she lost it a month later
to her sister-ship *Teutonic*.
1899 Dec: In service until March,
1900, as Boer War troop transport.
Two voyages to Cape Town.
1902 Alterations by Harland &
Wolff. New boilers, funnels
lengthened by 10 ft, and the two
after-masts replaced by one new
one. 10,147 GRT.
1903 Early in the year
Liverpool–New York service
again.
1907 Southampton–New York.
Jun 26: First voyage.
1911 Nov: Laid up.
1912 May: Re-entered service
following the loss of the *Titanic*.
1913 Oct 17: The *Majestic*
rescued the crew of the French
schooner *Garonne*.
1914 Sold to T. W. Ward for
breaking-up.
May 10: Arrival in Morecambe,
where she was broken up.

1 *The express steamer* Majestic *and
her sister-ship* Teutonic *were the
White Star Line's last
record-breakers. The* Majestic's
*appearance after alterations in
1902/3. The* Teutonic *was similarly
altered in 1913 without crossing the
10,000 GRT limit. She was broken up
at Emden in 1921.*

1

The M-Class of the P & O Line

Steamship *Marmora*
P & O Line, Belfast

Builders: Harland & Wolff,
Belfast
Yard no: 350
10,509 GRT; 166.3 × 18.4 m /
546 × 60.3 ft; IV exp eng, H & W;
Twin screw; 15,000 IHP; 17, max
18.5 kn; Passengers: 337 1st class,
187 2nd class; Crew: 370.

1903 Apr 9: Launched.
Nov: Completed.
Dec: Maiden voyage
London–Bombay.
1904 Mar 18: First voyage
London–Sydney.
1914 Aug: Auxiliary cruiser in
Royal Navy; 10th Cruiser
Squadron.
1918 Jul 23: The *Marmora* was
torpedoed and sunk off the Irish
coast by the German submarine
UB 64. Ten dead.

Steamship *Macedonia*
P & O Line, Belfast

Builders: Harland & Wolff,
Belfast
Yard no: 355
10,512 GRT; 177.4 × 18.4 m /
545 × 60.4 ft; IV exp eng, H & W;
Twin screw; 15,000 IHP; 17, max
18.5 kn; Passengers: 377 1st class,
187 2nd class; Crew: 370.

1903 Apr 11: Launched.
1904 Jan: Completed.
Feb 12: Maiden voyage
London–Bombay.
Apr 29: First voyage
London–Sydney.
1914 Aug: Auxiliary cruiser in
Royal Navy.
1915 Troop transport.
1916 Sold to British Admiralty.
1920 Bought back by P & O Line.
1921 After refitting,
London–Bombay–Far East
service. 11,089 GRT.
1922 Nov 24: One voyage
London–Sydney.
1931 Sold for breaking-up in
Japan.

1 *The* Marmora, *the first 10,000 tonner in the M-class of P & O.*
2 *The steamship* Macedonia *was one of the most successful British auxiliary cruisers during the opening months of the First World War.*

Steamship *Morea*
P & O Line, Glasgow

Builders: Barclay, Curle & Co, Glasgow
Yard no: 471
10,890 GRT; 171.3 × 18.5 m / 562 × 61.2 ft; IV exp eng from hull builders; Twin screw; 15,000 IHP; 17, max 18 kn; Passengers: 407 1st class, 200 2nd class; Crew: 307.

1908 Aug 15: Launched.
Nov 5: Completed.
Dec 4: Maiden voyage.
London–Sydney.
1915 Served as hospital ship.
1916 Troop transport.
1917 Apr: Auxiliary cruiser in Royal Navy.
1919 Oct 18: First postwar voyage London–Sydney. After six round-the-world trips, she served on the London–Bombay–Far East route.
1935 Sold for breaking-up in Yokohama.

Steamship *Malwa*
P & O Line, Greenock

Builders: Caird, Greenock
Yard no: 315
10,883 GRT; 170.7 × 18.7 m / 560 × 61.3 ft; IV exp eng; Caird; Twin screw; 15,000 IHP; 17, max 18 kn; Passengers: 400 1st class, 200 2nd class; Crew: 376.

1908 Oct 10: Launched.
Dec: Completed.
1909 Jan 29: Maiden voyage London–Sydney.
1917 Troop transport.
1920 Sep 24: First postwar voyage London–Sydney. Later on London–India–Far East route.
1932 May: Sold to shipbreakers in Japan.

3 The *Morea* *which entered the London–Sydney service in 1908.*
4 *P & O liner* Malwa. *Until the 'thirties, the superstructures of P & O passenger steamers were painted a dark yellowish brown.*

3

4

Steamship *Mantua*
P & O Line, Greenock

Builders: Caird, Greenock
Yard no: 316
10,885 GRT; 170.7 × 18.7 m /
560 × 61.3 ft; IV exp eng, Caird;
Twin screw; 15,000 IHP; 17, max
18 kn; Passengers: 400 1st class,
200 2nd class; Crew: 375.

1909 Feb 20: Launched.
Apr: Completed.
Jun 4: Maiden voyage
London–Sydney.
1913 Used mainly for cruising
until 1914.
1914 Aug 5: Served as auxiliary
cruiser in 10th Cruiser Squadron.
Later a troop transport.
1920 Jan 3: First postwar voyage
London–Sydney. Later on
London–India–Far East route.
1935 Broken up in Shanghai.

Steamship *Maloja*
P & O Line, Belfast

Builders: Harland & Wolff,
Belfast
Yard no: 414
12,431 GRT; 173.7 × 19.1 m /
625 × 62.9 ft; IV exp eng, H & W;
Twin screw; 16,000 IHP; 18, max
19.5 kn; Passengers: 450 1st class,
220 2nd class; Crew: 400.

1910 Dec 17: Launched.
1911 Sep 9: Completed.
Sep: Maiden voyage — a cruise to
the Hebrides.
1912 Feb 9: First voyage
London–Sydney.
1916 Feb 27: The *Maloja* struck a
mine two nautical miles off Dover
and sank. 122 dead.

Steamship *Medina*
P & O Line, Greenock

Builders: Caird, Greenock
Yard no: 317
12,350 GRT; 173.7 × 19.1 m /
625 × 62.9 ft; IV exp eng, Caird;
Twin screw; 16,000 IHP; 18, max
19.5 kn; Passengers: 460 1st class,
220 2nd class; Crew: 400.

1911 Mar 14: Launched.
Oct: Completed.
Nov 11: Maiden voyage
Portsmouth–Bombay as Royal
Yacht carrying King George V
and Queen Mary.
1912 Jun 28: First voyage
London–Sydney.
1917 Apr 28: The *Medina* was
torpedoed and sunk three nautical
miles east-northeast of Start Point
by the German submarine UB 31.
Six dead.

5

6

7

8

5/6 *The* Mantua *also was an auxiliary cruiser during the First World War.*
7 *The* Maloja, *a somewhat enlarged version of the M-class, entered service in 1911.*
8 *The* Medina *made her maiden voyage to Bombay in Nov 1911 as a British Royal Yacht. For this purpose, with other alterations, she was painted white and given an extra mast.*
9 *In 1912 the* Medina *made her first voyage to Australia in the traditional P & O colours.*

9

Minnesota and Dakota

Steamship: *Minnesota*
Great Northern SS Co, New York

1919 *Troy;* 1919 *Minnesota*

Builders: Eastern Shipbuilding
Co, New London
Yard no: 1
20,602 GRT; 192.0 × 22.4 m /
630 × 73.5 ft; III exp eng; Midvale
Steel Co; Twin screw; 10,800
IHP; 14, max 17 kn; Passengers:
300 1st class, 2,400 steerage.

1903 Apr 16: Launched.
1904 Aug 20: Delivered.
1905 Jan 23: Maiden voyage in
Transpacific service, USA–Far
East. New measurement: 20,718
GRT.
1916 Sold to Atlantic Transport
Line, New York. New boilers
fitted by Union Iron Works, San
Francisco.
Sep 29: Trials.
1917 Feb 14: First voyage San
Francisco–New York.
Apr 25: First voyage New
York–Liverpool.
Later, US Navy transport.
1919 Feb: Renamed *Troy*.
1919 Sep: Back to Atlantic
Transport Line as the *Minnesota*.
1920 North Atlantic service as
cargo vessel after removal of
passenger accommodation.
1923 Jun: Sold for breaking-up to
Merrit, Chapman & Scott
Wrecking Co.
Nov: Resold to Germany.
1924 Broken up in Germany.

Steamship *Dakota*
Great Northern SS Co, New York

Builders: Eastern Shipbuilding
Co, New London
Yard no: 2
20,714 GRT; 192.0 × 22.4 m /
630 × 73.5 ft; III exp eng, Midvale
Steel Co; Twin screw; 10,800
IHP; 14, max 17.5 kn; Passengers:
300 1st class, 2,400 steerage.

1904 Feb 7: Launched.
1905 Apr: Delivered.
Apr 28: First voyage New
York–Seattle.
Sep 20: Maiden voyage in
Transpacific service USA–Far
East.
1907 Mar 7: The *Dakota* ran
aground 40 nautical miles from
Yokohama on a submerged reef.
Passengers and crew abandoned
ship.
Mar 23: The ship broke up during a
storm and had to be written off as a
total loss. The wreck was
scrapped on the spot.

1/2 *The* Minnesota *(1) and her sister-ship* Dakota *(2) remained for 25 years the largest ships ever built in the USA.*
3 *The* Dakota *after running aground off Yokohama. Fortunately there was no loss of life in the accident. However, only a very small part of the valuable cargo could be salvaged.*

1

2

3

The Presidents Grant and Lincoln

Steamship *President Lincoln*
Hamburg–America Line,
Hamburg

Ex-*Scotian*

Builders: Harland & Wolff,
Belfast
Yard no: 353
18,168 GRT; 187.8 × 20.8 m /
616 × 68.2 ft; IV exp eng, H & W;
Twin screw; 7,650 IHP; 14.5 kn;
Passengers: 324 1st class, 152 2nd
class, 1,004 3rd class, 2,348
steerage; Crew: 344.

1903 Oct 8: Launched as *Scotian*.
The *Scotian* and her sister-ship
Servian had been ordered in 1902
by the British Wilson's &
Furness-Leyland Line, but the
company withdrew from the
contract while the ships were
being built. The yard launched the
ships and laid them up incomplete.
1906 Dec: Bought by
Hamburg-America Line.
Intended name *Berlin*.
1907 May 20: Completed as
President Lincoln.
Jun 1: Maiden voyage
Hamburg–New York.
1914 Aug: Interned in New York.
1917 Apr 6: Seized. Became US

Navy transport.
1918 May 31: On a voyage from
Europe to USA the *President
Lincoln* was torpedoed and sunk
by the German submarine U 90 in
a position 47°57′ N – 15°11′ W. 26
dead.

Steamship *President Grant*
Hamburg-America Line,
Hamburg

Ex-*Servian*; 1924 *Republic*

Builders: Harland & Wolff,
Belfast
Yard no: 354
18,072 GRT; 187.8 × 20.8 m /
616 × 68.2 ft; IV exp eng, H & W;
Twin screw; 7,650 IHP; 14.5 kn;
Passengers: 326 1st class, 152 2nd
class, 1,004 3rd class, 2,348
steerage; Crew: 350

1903 Dec 19: Launched as
Servian (see details of sister-ship).
1906 Dec: Bought by
Hamburg-America Line.
Intended name *Boston*.
1907 Aug 8: Completed as
President Grant.
Sep 14: Maiden voyage

Hamburg–New York.
1914 Aug: Interned in New York.
1917 Apr 6: Seized. US Navy
transport.
1921 Mar: Taken over by US
Shipping Board. Laid up at
Norfolk, Va.
1923 Until 1924 being
reconstructed at Newport News.
Third and fourth masts removed,
bridge section joined up with rest
of superstructure. Passengers: 619
cabin class, 1,332 3rd class. 17,910
GRT.
1924 Renamed *Republic*. While
she was being reconstructed the
intention had been to rename her
President Buchanan.
Apr 29: First voyage for United
States Lines, New
York–Hamburg.
1931 Aug: Taken over by US
Army as troop transport.
1941 Jun: Handed over to US
Navy, Transport AP 33.
1945 Jan: Sent to Mobile. Fitted
out there as hospital ship.
Aug: Served as US Army hospital
ship. Managed by Waterman SS
Co. 19,144 GRT.
1946 Feb: Troop transport again.
1951 Sold for breaking-up.
1952 Scrapped.

2

1 *The steamship*
President Lincoln *was
seized in New York in
1917, and as a US Navy*
*transport (in (2)
pictured before setting
out on her last voyage)
was sunk in 1918 by a
German submarine.*
3 *The Hamburg-
America liner*
President Grant. *The
two 'Presidents' were
the world's only large
liners to have six
masts.*
4 *The* Republic,
*ex-*President Grant,
*after her 1923
reconstruction.*

3

4

Caronia and Carmania

Steamship *Caronia*
Cunard Line, Liverpool

1932 Taiseiyo Maru

Builders: Brown, Clydebank
Yard no: 362
19,594 GRT; 206.6 × 22.0 m /
678 × 72.2 ft; IV exp eng, Brown;
Twin screw; 22,000 IHP; 18, max
20 kn; Passengers: 300 1st class,
350 2nd class, 900 3rd class, 1,100
steerage; Crew: 700.

1904 Jul 13: Launched.
1905 Feb: Completed.
Feb 25: Maiden voyage
Liverpool–New York.
1906 19,687 GRT.
1914 Aug 8: Auxiliary cruiser.
1916 Troop transport.
1919 Jan 11: First postwar voyage
Liverpool–New York.
1922 Hamburg–New York
service.
1923 Liverpool–New York again.
1924 Refitted at Barrow.
Passengers: 425 cabin class, 365
tourist class, 650 3rd class; oil-
firing; 19,566 GRT.
Liverpool–Montreal service.
1925 Liverpool–Boston or New
York.
1926 London–New York service.
1931 Laid up at Sheerness.
1932 Jan: Sold to Hughes
Bolckow & Co for breaking-up.
Nov: Resold to Japanese
breakers. For the voyage to Japan
renamed *Taiseiyo Maru*.
1933 Mar: Arrived at Osaka and
broken up there.

Turbine steamer *Carmania*
Cunard Line, Liverpool

Builders: Brown, Clydebank
Yard no: 366
19,524 GRT; 205.7 × 22.0 m /
675 × 72.2 ft; Turbines, Brown;
Triple screw; 21,000 SHP; 18,
max 20 kn; Passengers: 300 1st
class, 350 2nd class, 900 3rd class,
1,100 steerage; Crew: 700.

1905 Feb 21: Launched.
Nov 16: Completed.
Dec 2: Maiden voyage
Liverpool–New York.
1913 Oct 9: Took part in *Volturno*
rescue operation (see page 26).
1914 Aug 14: Auxiliary cruiser.
Sep 14: The *Carmania* surprised
the German auxiliary cruiser *Cap
Trafalgar* while the latter was
bunkering off the Brazilian island
of Trinidad. After two hours of
fighting the German ship sank, the
survivors being taken aboard the
Eleonore Woermann. The badly
damaged *Carmania,* which had
lost nine men in the action, turned
away on fire.
1916 May: Troop transport.
1918 Dec 21: First postwar
voyage Liverpool–New York.
1923 Refitted at the yard of her
builders during the winter of
1923/4. Passengers: 425 cabin
class, 365 tourist class, 650 3rd
class. Oil-firing. 19,566 GRT.
1924 Liverpool–Montreal
service.
1926 London–New York service.
1931 Aug: Laid up at Sheerness.
1932 Mar: Sold for breaking-up to
Hughes, Bolckow & Co, Blyth.

1 *This 1919 photo shows the original
appearance of the Cunard liner
Caronia.*
2 *The* Caronia *after alterations in
1924 which included the renewal of
lifeboats and davits.*
3 *In contrast to her sister-ship
Caronia which was propelled by
quadruple expansion engines, the
Carmania (3) was turbine-driven. She
was the Cunard Line's first
turbine-steamer.*

1

2

3

Turbine steamer *Victorian*
Allan Line, Glasgow

1922 Marloch

Builders: Workman, Clark & Co,
Belfast
Yard no: 206
10,635 GRT; 164.6 × 18.4 m /
540 × 60.4 ft; Turbines from hull
builders; Triple screw; 15,000
SHP; 18, max 19.5 kn;
Passengers: 346 1st class, 344 2nd
class, 1,000 3rd class; Crew: 250.

1904 Aug 25: Launched.
1905 Mar 10: Completed.
May 23: Maiden voyage
Liverpool–St John, later to
Quebec and Montreal. The
Victorian was the first
turbine-ship on the North
Atlantic.
1914 Aug 20: Auxiliary cruiser.
From Jun 9 to Dec 7, 1917, served
with the 10th Cruiser Squadron.
1915 Oct 1: Purchase of the Allan
Line by Canadian Pacific.
1920 Jan 31: Released from naval
service. Liverpool–Canada
service.
1921 Refitted by Fairfield,
Glasgow. New geared
turbines. 7,500 SHP, 14.5 kn;
Passengers: 418 cabin class, 566
3rd class. 10,687 GRT.
1922 Dec 11: Renamed *Marloch*.
1925 Up to 1929 used
occasionally as reserve ship on
Canadian service; laid up several
times for months on end.
1929 Apr 5: Sold for breaking-up
to T. W. Ward.
Apr 17: Arrived in Milford Haven
and scrapped there.

Turbine steamer *Virginian*
Allan Line, Glasgow

1920 Drottningholm; *1948 Brasil*;
1951 Homeland

Builders: Stephen, Glasgow
Yard no: 405
10,754 GRT; 164.0 × 18.4 m /
538 × 60.3 ft; Turbines, Parsons;
Triple screw; 15,000 SHP; 18, max
19.8 kn; Passengers: 426 1st class,
286 2nd class, 1,000 3rd class;
Crew: 250.

1904 Dec 22: Launched
1905 Mar 31: Completed.
Apr 6: Maiden voyage
Liverpool–St John, later to
Montreal.
1914 Aug: Troop transport.
Nov 13: Auxiliary cruiser with
10th Cruiser Squadron.
1915 Oct 1: Purchase of the Allan
Line by Canadian Pacific.
1920 Jan 31: Released from naval
service.
Feb 14: Sold to
Swedish-American Line,
Gothenburg. Renamed
Drottningholm.
May: First voyage

Gothenburg–New York.
1922 Until 1923, being
reconstructed by Götaverken.
New De Laval geared turbines.
10,500 SHP. 17, max 18.25 kn;
Passengers: 532 cabin class, 854
3rd class; 11,182 GRT.
1940 In the service of the
International Red Cross until
1946. Facilitated exchanges of
prisoners and wounded between
the combatant powers.
1945 Sold to Home Lines,
Panama. Delivered in 1948.
1948 Jul 27: First voyage
Genoa–South America for Home
Lines under the new name *Brasil*.
1950 Naples–New York service.
1951 Reconstructed in Italy.
10,043 GRT. Passengers: 96 1st
class, 846 tourist class. Renamed
Homeland.
Jun 16: First voyage
Hamburg–New York. On this
service until 1952 under the
management of the
Hamburg-America Line.
1952 Genoa–New York service.
1955 Mar 29: Arrived in Trieste.
Broken-up by 'Sidarma'.

2

3

4

1 *The Allan Liner* Victorian *was the first turbine steamer on the North Atlantic.*
2 *The* Marloch, *ex*-Victorian. *The Allan Line was taken over in 1915 by Canadian Pacific, who gave her this new name.*
3 *The Allan Line's turbine steamer* Virginian.
4 *Sold to the Swedish-American Line in 1920, the* Virginian *was renamed* Drottningholm.

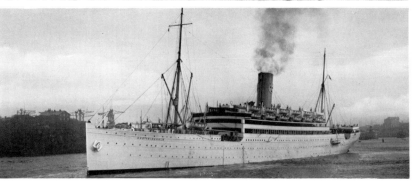

Steamship *Corsican*
Allan Line, Glasgow

1922 Marvale

Builders: Barclay, Curle and Co,
Glasgow
Yard no: 467
11,436 GRT; 157.3 × 18.7 m /
516 × 61.2 ft; III exp eng from hull
builders; Twin screw; 9,500 IHP;
16, max 17.4 kn; Passengers: 208
1st class, 298 2nd class, 1,000 3rd
class.

1907 Apr 29: Launched.
Nov: Completed. Maiden voyage
Liverpool–St John.
1914 Glasgow–Montreal service.
Aug 8: Troop transport.
1915 Oct 1: Purchase of Allan
Line by Canadian Pacific.
1922 Reconstructed in Liverpool
as cabin class ship.
Nov 16: Renamed *Marvale*.
1923 May 21: Stranded on Freel
Rock 20 nautical miles west of
Cape Race. Total loss.

Steamship *Grampian*
Allan Line, Glasgow

Builders: Stephen, Glasgow
Yard no: 422
10,187 GRT; 153.0 × 18.3 m /
502 × 60.2 ft; III exp eng,
Stephen; Twin screw; 7,700 IHP;
15, max 15.8 kn; Passengers: 210
1st class, 250 2nd class, 1,000 3rd
class.

1907 Jul 25: Launched.
Dec: Completed. Maiden voyage
Glasgow–Montreal. Tonnage,
according to Lloyd's register:
1908: 9,603 GRT;
1909: 10,187 GRT;
1910: 10,947 GRT.
1915 Oct 1: Purchase of Allan
Line by Canadian Pacific.
1921 Mar: Badly damaged by fire
in Antwerp; condemned.
1925 Sold for breaking-up to F.
Rijsdijk, Hendrik-Ido-Ambacht.

Steamship *Hesperian*
Allan Line, Glasgow

Builders: Stephen, Glasgow
Yard no: 425
10,920 GRT; 153.0 × 18.3 m /
502 × 60.2 ft; III exp eng;
Stephen; Twin screw; 8,200 IHP;
15, max 16.5 kn; Passengers: 210
1st class, 250 2nd class, 1,000 3rd
class.

1907 Dec 20: Launched.
1908 Apr 16: Delivered.
Apr 25: Maiden voyage
Glasgow–Montreal.
1915 Sep 4: The *Hesperian* was
torpedoed and sunk 85 nautical
miles southwest of Fastnet by the
German submarine U 20. 32 dead.

5 *In her later years, the ex-*Virginian
*sailed from 1948 onwards for Home
Lines under the names* Brasil *and*
Homeland.

6

7

8

6 *As the* Marvale, *the former* Corsican *stranded off Cape Race in 1923.*
7/8 *The Allan Liners* Grampian *(7) and* Hesperian *(8) both came to early ends. The* Grampian *was burnt out in 1921, and the* Hesperian *sunk by a German submarine in 1915.*

The Amerika-Class

Steamship *Amerika*
Hamburg-America Line,
Hamburg

1917 *America*; 1941 *Edmund B. Alexander*

Builders: Harland & Wolff,
Belfast
Yard no: 357
22,225 GRT; 213.4 × 22.7 m /
700 × 74.3 ft; IV exp eng, H & W;
Twin screw; 16,500 IHP; 17.5,
max 18 kn; Passengers: 420 1st
class, 254 2nd class, 223 3rd class,
1,765 steerage; Crew: 577.

1905 Apr 20: Launched.
Sep 21: Completed.
Oct 11: Maiden voyage
Hamburg–New York. Until 1906
the largest ship in the world.
1907 New measurement: 22,622
GRT.
1912 Oct 4: Off Dover the
Amerika rammed the British
submarine B 2 which immediately
sank. 15 dead. One man rescued.
1914 Jun 10: First voyage
Hamburg–Boston.
Aug: Interned in Boston.
1917 Apr 6: Seized. Renamed
America.
Oct 31: US Navy transport.
1918 Jul 14: In collision with
British steamer *Instructor,* which
sank with the loss of 16 lives.
Oct 15: Sank in New York due to
bad trimming when taking on coal.
Six dead.
Dec 12: Raised. Repaired by New
York Navy Yard.
1919 Feb 21: Back in service.
Sep 26: Laid up by US Shipping
Board.
1920 May: Overhaul and refitting
until June, 1921, in Brooklyn by
Morse Dry Dock & Repair Co.
1921 Jun 22: First voyage in New

York–Europe service on charter
to US Mail SS Co.
Aug: To United States Lines,
New York–Bremerhaven route.
1923 Reconstructed in Brooklyn
Navy Yard. 21,114 GRT.
1926 Mar 10: Badly damaged in
a large fire while refitting at
Newport News. Breaking-up
considered.
1927 Repaired by Newport News
Shipbuilding & Dry Dock Co.
21,329 GRT.
1931 Laid up in Chesapeake Bay.
1940 Oct: To Baltimore for
conversion to accommodation
ship by the Bethlehem Steel Corp.
1941 Jan: Renamed *Edmund B.
Alexander.* Accommodation ship
for the US Maritime Commission
in St Johns, Newfoundland.
Jun: Fitted out as troop transport
at Atlantic Basin Iron Works,
New York. Transport service
between New Orleans and
Panama.
1942 May: US Maritime
Commission decided on a general
overhaul of the engines, which
were giving only 10 kn. Bethlehem
Steel Corp in Baltimore carried
out the work. Conversion to
oil-firing. Removal of one funnel.
1943 Apr: US Army transport.
1949 May 26: Laid up in
Baltimore.
1957 Jan 27: Arrival in Baltimore
for breaking-up by Bethlehem
Steel Corp.
1958 Scrapped.

1

2

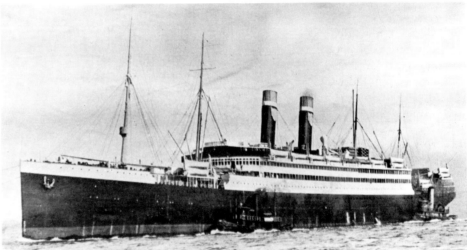

3

1 *The Hamburg-America liner* Amerika *led an eventful life until she was broken up at the age of 53. She rammed and sank two ships, herself sank, once was almost burnt out, sailed as a passenger liner for three owners and as a troop transport in two world wars.*
2 *The* America *in 1921 with the funnel-markings of the short-lived US Mail Steamship Co.*
3 *After 1943, the troop transport* Edmund B. Alexander, *ex-*Amerika, *had only one funnel. In this photograph the ship is being towed to the breakers' yard.*

Steamship *Kaiserin Auguste Victoria*
Hamburg-America Line, Hamburg

1921 *Empress of Scotland*

Builders: 'Vulcan', Stettin
Yard no: 264
24,581 GRT; 214.9 × 23.5 m /
705 × 77.3 ft; IV exp eng, Vulcan;
Twin screw; 17,500 IHP; 17.5,
max 18 kn; Passengers: 652 1st
class, 286 2nd class, 216 3rd class,
1,842 steerage; Crew: 593.

1905 Aug 29: Launched. Intended name *Europa*.
1906 Apr 28: Completed.
May 10: Maiden voyage Hamburg–New York. Until 1907 the largest ship in the world.
1914 Aug: Laid up in Hamburg for duration of war.
1919 Mar 23: Handed over to Great Britain. Chartered to the US Shipping Board by the Shipping Controller. Troop transport.
1920 Feb 14: First voyage Liverpool–New York under charter to Cunard.
1921 May 13: Sold to Canadian Pacific Railway Co, London.
Aug 5: Renamed *Empress of Scotland*. Refitted by Vulcan-Werft, Hamburg. Converted to oil-firing.
Passengers: 459 1st class, 478 2nd class, 536 3rd class; 25,037 GRT.
1922 Jan 22: First voyage Southampton–New York, then Southampton–Quebec. Cruising.
1930 Dec 2: Sold for breaking-up to Hughes, Bolckow & Co, Blyth.
Dec 10: Completely burnt out at Blyth. Sank.
1931 May: Raised.
Jun 1: The wreck broke apart while being moved. Scrapped.

4 Kaiserin Auguste Victoria *of the Hamburg-America Line took over from the* Amerika *as the largest ship in the world.*
5 *Canadian Pacific Liner* Empress of Scotland, *ex-*Kaiserin Auguste Victoria.

4

5

Steamship *George Washington*
North German Lloyd, Bremen

1941 *Catlin*;
1941 *George Washington*

Builders: 'Vulcan', Stettin
Yard no: 286
25,570 GRT; 220.2 × 23.8 m /
723 × 72.8 ft; IV exp eng, Vulcan;
Twin screw; 22,000 IHP; 18.5,
max 20 kn; Passengers: 568 1st
class, 433 2nd class, 452 3rd class,
1,226 steerage; Crew: 585.

1908 Nov 10: Launched.
1909 Jun 2: Completed.
Jun 12: Maiden voyage
Bremerhaven–New York.
1914 Aug: Interned in New York.
1917 Apr 6: Seized. US Navy
transport.
1919 Handed over to US Army as
troop transport.

1920 Jan: To US Shipping Board.
Laid up at Boston.
Oct: Chartered to US Mail Lines,
New York. Refitted and
overhauled by Tietjen & Lang.
New York. 23,788 GRT.
1921 Aug 3: First voyage New
York–Bremen.
Aug: Taken over by United States
Lines; same service.
1931 Nov: Laid-up from 1932 on
the Patuxent River.
1940 Again in service as US
Navy transport.
1941 Renamed *Catlin*. Placed at
disposal of British Ministry of War
Transport. Renamed *George
Washington*.
1942 Feb: Handed back to US
Maritime Commission because of
the condition of the boilers.
Jun: After a few New

York–Panama voyages, during
which the ship could manage
scarcely 11 kn, she was sent for
alterations to Todd's Brooklyn
Yard. New boilers, oil-firing, one
funnel.
1943 Following these changes,
US Army transport.
1947 Mar: Badly damaged by fire
in New York. Laid up in
Baltimore.
1951 Jan 17: Completely
destroyed by a large fire which
spread from the quay to the ship.
The wreck scrapped.

6

7

8

9

6/7 *The* George Washington, *North German Lloyd's biggest ship prior to the First World War.*
8 *A 1918 photo: US Navy transport* George Washington.
9 *In the 'twenties, the* George Washington *sailed between New York and Bremen for United States Lines.*

Nieuw Amsterdam and Rotterdam

Steamship *Nieuw Amsterdam*
Holland–America Line,
Rotterdam

Builders: Harland & Wolff,
Belfast
Yard no: 366
16,967 GRT; 187.4 × 20.9 m /
615 × 68.0 ft; IV exp eng, H & W;
Twin screw; 10,400 IHP; 16 kn;
Passengers: 440 1st class, 246 2nd
class, 2,200 3rd class.

1905 Sep 28: Launched.
1906 Feb 22: Completed.
Apr 7: Maiden voyage
Rotterdam–New York.
1910 17,149 GRT after alterations
by Harland & Wolff. Passengers:
443 1st class, 379 2nd class, 2,050
3rd class.
1926 Passengers: 300 1st class,
860 tourist class.
1932 Feb 26: Sailed from
Rotterdam for breaking-up in
Osaka.

Steamship *Rotterdam*
Holland–America Line,
Rotterdam

Builders: Harland & Wolff,
Belfast
Yard no: 390
24,149 GRT; 203.2 × 23.7 m /
667 × 77.4 ft; IV exp eng, H & W;
Twin screw; 15,000 IHP; 17 kn;
Passengers: 520 1st class, 555 2nd
class, 2,500 3rd class.

1908 Mar 3: Launched.
Jun 3: Completed.
Jun 13: Maiden voyage
Rotterdam–New York.
1916 Laid up in Rotterdam
because of the war and danger
from mines.

1919 Feb: First postwar voyage
Rotterdam–New York.
1923 Refit with conversion to
oil-firing. Passengers: 550 1st
class, 555 2nd class, 808 tourist
class. Again considerably
reduced during the 'thirties.
1939 Dec: Sold for breaking-up.
1940 Broken-up by F. Rijsdijk in
Hendrik-Ido-Ambacht.

1/2 The Nieuw Amsterdam, *flagship
of the Holland-America Line when
commissioned, pictured (above) in her
first years of service, and (below) after
reconstruction in 1910.*
3/4 *The Holland-America liner*
Rotterdam *was the first Transatlantic
steamer to have a glass-enclosed
promenade deck.*

1

2

Two Empresses

Steamship *Empress of Britain*
Canadian Pacific, Liverpool

1924 *Montroyal*

Builders: Fairfield, Glasgow
Yard no: 442
14,189 GRT; 173.7 × 20.0 m /
570 × 65.7 ft; IV exp eng,
Fairfield; Twin screw; 18,800
IHP; 18, max 19.8 kn; Passengers:
310 1st class, 500 2nd class, 500 3rd
class, 270 steerage.
1905 Nov 11: Launched.
1906 Apr: Completed.
May 5: Maiden voyage
Liverpool–Quebec.
1912 Jul 27: Collided in fog with
British steamer *Helvetia* off Cape
Madeleine. The *Helvetia* sank.
1914 Aug 16: Auxiliary cruiser.
1915 May: Troop transport.
1919 Mar 21: Back to Canadian
Pacific.
Aug: Refitted by Fairfield with
conversion to oil-firing.
1924: Refit: Passengers: 600 cabin
class, 800 3rd class, 15,646 GRT.
Apr 16: Renamed *Montroyal*.
1927 Antwerp–Canada service,
occasionally from Hamburg.
1929 Laid up off Southend.
1930 Jun 17: Sold for breaking-up
to Stavanger Shipbreaking Co.

Steamship *Empress of Ireland*
Canadian Pacific, Liverpool

Builders: Fairfield, Glasgow
Yard no: 443
14,191 GRT; 173.7 × 20.0 m /
570 × 65.7 ft; IV exp eng,
Fairfield; Twin screw; 19,000
IHP; 18, max 20 kn; Passengers:
310 1st class, 500 2nd class, 500 3rd
class, 270 steerage.

1906 Jan 27: Launched.
Jun 5: Completed.
Jun 29: Maiden voyage
Liverpool–Quebec.
1914 May 29: The *Empress of
Ireland* was rammed in thick fog
on the St Lawrence River near
Father Point by the Norwegian
steamer *Storstad*. The *Empress*
began to sink immediately. The
disaster claimed 1,024 lives.

3 *This memorial was erected by
Canadian Pacific at the burial place of
the recovered victims of the* Empress
of Ireland *disaster. The accident
claimed a total of 1,024 lives.*

1

2

1 *The Canadian Pacific Liner*
Empress of Britain *was renamed*
Montroyal *in 1924.*

2 *The* Empress of Ireland *fell victim
to one of the worst-ever shipping
disasters. She was rammed by the
Norwegian steamer* Storstad *and
sank very rapidly.*

Steamship *Amazon*
Royal Mail Lines, Belfast

Builders: Harland & Wolff,
Belfast
Yard no: 372
10,037 GRT; 161.5 × 18.4 m /
530 × 60.4 ft; IV exp eng, H & W;
Twin screw; 8,000 IHP; 16, max
16.5 kn; Passengers: 300 1st class;
70 2nd class; 500 3rd class.

1906 Feb 24: Launched.
Jun 14: Delivered.
Jun 15: Maiden voyage
Southampton–La Plata ports.
1918 Mar 15: Torpedoed and sunk
off the north coast of Ireland near
Malin Head by the German
submarine U 52.

Steamship *Araguaya*
Royal Mail Lines, Belfast

1930 *Kraljica Marija*; 1940 *Savoie*

Builders: Workman, Clark & Co,
Belfast
Yard no: 230
10,537 GRT; 162.1 × 18.7 m /
532 × 61.3 ft; IV exp eng from hull
builders; Twin screw; 8,000 IHP;
16 kn; Passengers: 285 1st class,
100 2nd class, 800 3rd class.

1906 Jun 5: Launched.
Sep: Completed.
Southampton–La Plata service.
1917 Fitted out as hospital ship.
1920 Back to Royal Mail Lines,
refitted as passenger vessel.
1920 Oct 29: First postwar
voyage, Southampton–La Plata.
1926 Re-built in Belfast as
cruise-ship, 365 1st class
passengers. 10,196 GRT.
1930 Nov 11: To Jugoslavenski
Lloyd, Dubrovnik. Renamed
Kraljica Marija. Employed in
Mediterranean and Black Sea.
1940 Sold to French Government
and renamed *Savoie*. South
America service under CGT
management.
1942 Nov 8: Sunk off Casablanca
during the Allied landings in North
Africa.

Steamship *Avon*
Royal Mail Lines, Belfast

1916 *Avoca*; 1917 *Avon*

Builders: Harland & Wolff,
Belfast
Yard no: 382
11,073 GRT; 163.1 × 19.0 m /
535 × 62.3 ft; IV exp eng, H & W;
Twin screw; 8,500 IHP; 16 kn;
Passengers: 300 1st class, 140 2nd
class, 1,200 3rd class.

1907 Mar 2: Launched.
Jun: Completed.
Jun 28: Maiden voyage
Southampton–La Plata.
1914 Aug: Troop transport.
1915 Jan: Auxiliary cruiser in
Royal Navy, renamed *Avoca*.
1917 Troop transport, original
name, *Avon*, restored.
1919 Nov: First postwar voyage
Southampton–La Plata. Mainly
employed on cruising during the
'twenties.
1927 Hull painted white.
1929 Sep: Laid up in
Southampton.
1930 Jan: Sold to T. W. Ward and
broken-up at Briton Ferry.

1

2

3

1 *Royal Mail Lines put nine ships of the famous A-class into service in the ten years between 1905 and 1914. Pictured here is the* Amazon, *which entered service in 1906 and was Royal Mail's first 10,000 tonner. The sister-ship* Aragon, *9,441 GRT, which had entered service a year earlier, fell victim to a German submarine in the Mediterranean on Dec 30, 1917, while she was serving as a troop transport. 610 lives were lost.*
2 *Jugoslavenski Lloyd's* Kraljica Marija, *which was built in 1906 for Royal Mail Lines as the* Araguaya.
3 *The* Avon *served as an auxiliary cruiser in World War I under the name* Avoca.

Steamship *Asturias*
Royal Mail Lines, Belfast

1923 *Arcadian*

Builders: Harland & Wolff,
Belfast
Yard no: 388
12,002 GRT; 163.1 × 19.0 m /
535 × 62.3 ft; IV exp eng, H & W;
Twin screw; 8,500 IHP; 16 kn;
Passengers: 300 1st class, 140 2nd
class, 1,200 3rd class.

1907 Sep 26: Launched.
1908 Jan: Completed.
Jan 24: Maiden voyage
London–Brisbane. Then
Southampton–La Plata service.
1914 Aug: Served as hospital
ship.
1917 Mar 20: Torpedoed by
German submarine in English
Channel. 35 dead. The
unmanoeuvrable ship was run
ashore off Bolt Head and
abandoned to underwriters as a
total loss. The British Admiralty
bought the wreck. After salvage
work lasting several months she
was towed to Plymouth and used
there as a munitions hulk.
1919 Sold to Royal Mail Lines.
Towed to Belfast and laid up
there.
1922 Repaired by Harland &
Wolff, and fitted out for cruising.
1923 Jun 3: After completion of
refit entered service under the new
name of *Arcadian*. Cruising.
1930 Oct: Laid up at
Southampton.
1933 Feb: Sold for breaking-up in
Japan.

Steamship *Arlanza*
Royal Mail Lines, Belfast

Builders: Harland & Wolff,
Belfast
Yard no: 415
15,044 GRT; 179.5 × 19.9 m /
589 × 65.3; III exp eng plus
low pressure turbine, H & W;
triple screw; 14,000 IHP; 17 kn;
Passengers: 400 1st class, 230 2nd
class, 760 3rd class.

1911 Nov 23: Launched.
1912 Jun 8: Completed.
Sep: Maiden voyage
Southampton–La Plata.
1915 Apr: Auxiliary cruiser with
10th Cruiser Squadron.
1920 Jul 27: First postwar voyage
Southampton–La Plata.
1938 Sold for breaking-up to
Hughes, Bolckow & Co, Blyth.

4 The Asturias *was rebuilt in 1922/23
to become the cruise liner* Arcadian.
*This photo shows her in Hamburg
harbour.*
5 The Arlanza, *first ship of the second
larger and faster A-class series, was
completed in 1912.*

4

5

Steamship *Andes*
Royal Mail Lines, Liverpool

1930 *Atlantis*

Builders: Harland & Wolff, Belfast
Yard no: 434
15,620 GRT; 179.5 × 20.5 m / 589 × 67.3 ft; III exp eng plus low pressure turbine, H & W; Triple screw; 14,000 IHP; 17 kn; Passengers: 380 1st class, 250 2nd class, 700 3rd class.

1913 May 8: Launched. The ship was intended for the Pacific Steam Navigation Co, but taken over by Royal Mail Lines before launching.
Sep 11: Completed.
Sep 26: Maiden voyage Liverpool–Chile for Pacific Steam Navigation Co, then Southampton–La Plata service for Royal Mail Lines.
1915 Apr: Auxiliary cruiser with 10th Cruiser Squadron.
1916 Feb 29: The *Andes* and her sister-ship *Alcantara* engaged the German auxiliary cruiser *Greif* in the northern North Sea between the Shetlands and the Norwegian coast. *Alcantara* and *Greif* were sunk in the action. The *Andes* rescued the survivors of both ships.
1919 Nov 4: First postwar voyage Southampton–La Plata.
1930 Fitted out as a cruise liner in Liverpool. 450 1st class passengers, 15,135 GRT. White hull. Oil-firing. Renamed *Atlantis*.
1939 Sep: Sold to British government to become a hospital ship; managed by Royal Mail Lines.
1948 Reconstructed for emigrant service to Australia and New Zealand. 900 3rd class passengers, 15,363 GRT.
1952 Sold for breaking-up at Faslane.

Steamship *Alcantara*
Royal Mail Lines, Belfast

Builders: Harland & Wolff, Govan
Yard no: 435
15,831 GRT; 179.5 × 20.5 m / 589 × 67.3 ft; III exp eng with low pressure turbine, H & W; Triple screw; 14,000 IHP; 17 kn; Passengers: 400 1st class, 230 2nd class, 700 3rd class.

1913 Oct 30: Launched.
1914 May 29: Completed.
Jun 19: Maiden voyage Southampton–La Plata.
1915 Apr: Auxiliary cruiser with 10th Cruiser Squadron.
1916 Feb 29: The *Alcantara* intercepted in the Skagerrak the German auxiliary cruiser *Greif* disguised as the Norwegian *Reno*. As the British lowered a boat with a prize crew, the *Greif* hoisted the German battle ensign and opened fire which the *Alcantara* returned. The ships being at a distance of little over 3,000 yds from each other, nearly every shot was on target: The British auxiliary cruiser *Andes* came to assist the *Alcantara,* but the latter began to sink after 30 minutes, and went down after a further half-hour. The burning and unmanoeuvrable *Greif* was sunk by the *Andes* with the cruiser *Comus* and destroyer *Munster,* which had arrived in the meantime. 69 of the *Alcantara's* company lost their lives in the action.

Steamship *Almanzora*
Royal Mail Lines, Belfast

Builders: Harland & Wolff, Belfast
Yard no: 441
16,034 GRT; 179.5 × 20.5 m / 589 × 67.3 ft; III exp eng plus low pressure turbine; Triple screw; 14,000 IHP; 17 kn; Passengers: 400 1st class, 230 2nd class, 760 3rd class.

1914 Nov 19: Launched.
1915 Sep: Completed as auxiliary cruiser.
Sep 29: 10th Cruiser Squadron.
1919 Jan 14: Released from naval service. Refitted as passenger ship by Harland & Wolff, 15,551 GRT.
1920 Jan 9: Maiden voyage Southampton–La Plata.
1939 Troop transport.
1947 Laid up in Cowes Roads.
1948 Sold to British Iron & Steel Corp; Broken up at Blyth.

6 *The* Andes *of 1913 was fitted out for cruising in 1930 and renamed* Atlantis. *At this time, her hull was painted white.*
7 *While serving as an auxiliary cruiser in the Royal Navy in 1916, the* Alcantara *engaged the German auxiliary cruiser* Greif, *in the course of which action both ships sank.*
8 *The last liner of the A-class, the* Almanzora *was completed in 1915 as an auxiliary cruiser; in 1919 she was reconstructed as a passenger ship.*

6

7

8

Lusitania and Mauretania

Turbine steamer *Lusitania*
Cunard Line, Liverpool

Builders: Brown, Clydebank
Yard no: 367
31,550 GRT; 239.9 × 26.7 m /
787 × 87.8 ft; Turbines, Brown;
Quadruple screw; 76,000 SHP; 25,
max 26.35 kn; Passengers: 563 1st
class, 464 2nd class, 1,138 3rd
class; Crew: 802.

1906 Jun 7: Launched.
1907 Aug 26: Delivered. At this
time, the largest ship in the world.
Sep 7: Maiden voyage
Liverpool–New York.
Oct: The *Lusitania* gained the
'Blue Riband' with an average
speed of 23.99 kn between
Queenstown and the Ambrose
Light. On the return voyage she
broke the West–East record with
23,61 kn. In May, 1908, she had to
surrender the 'Blue Riband' to
her sister-ship *Mauretania,* but
regained it from her in July. The
Lusitania made her fastest voyage
in 1909, when she averaged 25.85
kn from Daunts Rock to Sandy
Hook. In Sep, 1909, she lost her
record permanently to the
Mauretania.
1914 Aug: Originally intended as
an auxiliary cruiser in the event of
war, the *Lusitania* was not taken
over by the Royal Navy because
of her size and fuel consumption.
She remained on the
Liverpool–New York passenger
service. For reasons of economy,
six of the boilers were shut down,
reducing her speed to 21 kn.
1915 Feb 4: In a note to all
powers, the German government
declared the waters around Great
Britain and Ireland to be a
war-zone, in which all enemy

shipping found there from Feb 18,
1915, would be sunk.
May 1: The German Embassy in
Washington published a warning
in a New York newspaper which
was inserted next to a Cunard
advertisement. Travellers were
reminded of the German
declaration of Feb 4, and of the
dangers they faced in using Allied
ships.
May 1: The *Lusitania* left New
York bound for Liverpool. 1,959
people were on board, including
440 women and 129 children.
May 7: The ship reached the Irish
coast, and at mid-day was off the
Old Head of Kinsdale when she
was torpedoed by the German
submarine U 20. The *Lusitania*
immediately developed a list to
starboard and sank bow-first 20
minutes later. 1,198 people
perished. The survivors were
rescued by the trawler *Peel* and by
boats which had quickly set out
from the Irish coast. For the first
time in the history of sea warfare a
large passenger-ship had been
sunk by a submarine without
warning in an underwater attack.
In Great Britain the news was
received with horror and a
growing hate of the U-boats. The
neutral world reacted with disgust
and indignation. Germany
celebrated the sinking as a heroic
deed, but it should be noted that it
was reported to the German public
as the sinking of an armed
munitions and troop-transport.
That the *Lusitania* did in fact have
4,343 cases of ammunition on
board, officially declared, is only
relevant inasmuch as this
ammunition was accepted on the
German side as the reason for the

speed with which the ship sank,
and hence for the heavy loss of
life. The commander of the U 20
claimed to have fired only one
torpedo. Aboard the *Lusitania,*
however, there was a second
tremendous explosion after the
impact of the torpedo. In the
British view this was a second
torpedo, while the Germans
claimed that it was caused by the
ammunition cargo. Whatever the
cause might have been, the effect
was so devastating that the ship,
which had been sailing with most
of her bulkhead doors closed,
sank within 20 minutes.

The fate of the *Lusitania* was
one of the first examples of
modern 'total war'.

1/2 The Cunard liner Lusitania, *the
world's first 30,000 tonner on her
trials. The sinking of this ship by a
German submarine, whereby 1,198
people died, turned world opinion
against Germany.*

1

2

Turbine steamer *Mauretania*
Cunard Line, Liverpool

Builders: Swan Hunter & Wigham
Richardson, Newcastle
Yard no: 735
31,938 GRT; 240.8 × 26.8 m /
790 × 88.0 ft; Turbines, Wallsend
Slipway; Quadruple screw; 78,000
SHP; 25, max 26.75 kn;
Passengers: 560 1st class, 475 2nd
class, 1,300 3rd class; Crew: 812.

1906 Sep 20: Launched.
1907 Sep 17: First shipyard trials.
Nov 7: Delivered. Until 1911
largest ship in the world.
Nov 16: Maiden voyage
Liverpool–New York. On her
return voyage she broke the
record with 23.69 kn between
Ambrose and Queenstown. In
May, 1908, she broke the record
for the opposite direction, which
the *Lusitania* then took from her
for a few months once more. In
September, 1909, the *Mauretania*
covered the distance between
Daunts Rock and Sandy Hook
with an average speed of 26.06 kn,
and with this she held the 'Blue
Riband' unchallenged for 20
years. In July, 1929, the *Bremen*
broke this record. One month later
the *Mauretania,* now 22 years old,
entered the contest again but could
not beat the *Bremen,* recording
(the *Bremen's* figures in
parentheses) 26.9 kn (27.83) on the
westward run, and 27.22 kn (27.92)
eastward — a quite astonishing
achievement.
1915 Jun: Troop transport.
Sep: Hospital ship.
1916 Troop transport again.
1919 Jun 27: First postwar
voyage, Southampton–New
York.
1921 Jul 25: Severely damaged by
fire at Southampton. Repaired at
her builders' yard at Newcastle.
At the same time the passenger
accommodation was re-modelled
and the ship converted to
oil-firing. Passengers: 589 1st
class, 400 2nd class, 767 3rd class.
30,696 GRT.
1922 Mar 25: Southampton–New
York service again.
1930 Mainly used for cruising.
1933 May: Hull painted white.
1935 Apr: Sold for breaking-up.
Jul 4: Arrived in Rosyth; broken
up there by Metal Industries Ltd.

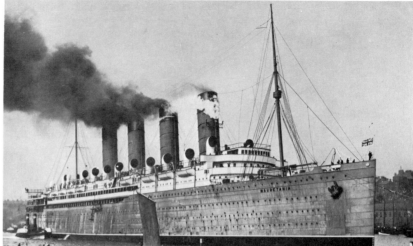

4

5

3

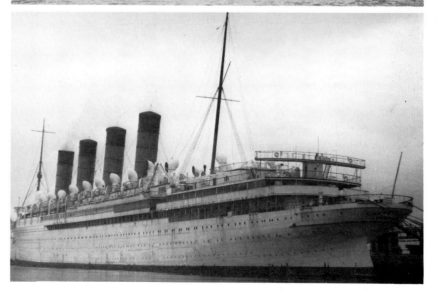

6

3 *The most famous express steamer of all time, the* Mauretania *before her launching.*
4 *Sep 1907: Departure of the* Mauretania *for her first trials. The hull still displays the protective grey paint, which, before her delivery, was overpainted black.*
5-7 *From 1930 the* Mauretania *was used mainly for cruising. In 1933 her hull was painted white.*

Heliopolis and Cairo

Turbine steamer *Heliopolis*
Egyptian Mail, London

1910 *Royal George*

Builders: Fairfield, Glasgow
Yard no: 449
10,897 GRT; 166.1 × 18.4 m /
545 × 60.2 ft; Turbines from hull
builders; Triple screw; 18,000
SHP; 19, max 20.7 kn;
Passengers: 710 1st class, 290 2nd
class.

1907 May 28: Launched.
Nov 6: Completed.
Marseille–Alexandria service;
unprofitable so discontinued after
a year.
1909 Laid up at Marseille and
offered for sale.
1910 Sold to Canadian Northern
Steamships, Toronto. Renamed
Royal George. Fitted out by
Fairfield for North Atlantic
service. 11,146 GRT.
May 26: First voyage
Avonmouth–Montreal.
1914 Troop transport.
1916 Cunard Line bought
Canadian Northern Steamships
and took over the *Royal George*.
1919 Feb 8: First postwar voyage
Liverpool–New York.
Aug 14: First voyage,
Southampton–New York.
1920 Jun: Accommodation ship at
Cherbourg.
1922 Jul: Sold for breaking-up at
the Wilhelmshaven navy yard.
Aug 7: Arrived at Wilhelmshaven.

Turbine steamer *Cairo*
Egyptian Mail, London

1910 *Royal Edward*

Builders: Fairfield, Glasgow
Yard no: 450
10,864 GRT; 166.1 × 18.4 m /
545 × 60.2 ft; Turbines from hull
builders; Triple screw; 18,000
SHP; 19, max 20.5 kn;
Passengers: 710 1st class, 290 2nd
class.

1907 Jul: Launched.
1908 Jan: Completed.
Marseille–Alexandria service,
unprofitable so discontinued after
a year.
1909 Laid up at Marseille and
offered for sale.
1910 Sold to Canadian Northern
Steamships, Toronto. Renamed
Royal Edward. Refitted by
Fairfield for North Atlantic
service. 11,117 GRT.
May 12: First voyage
Avonmouth–Montreal.
1914 Troop transport.
1915 Aug 14: The *Royal Edward*
was torpedoed and sunk in the
Aegean by the German submarine
UB 14. 935 dead.

1 *The* Heliopolis *and her sister-ship
could not compete in the
Mediterranean against the
old-established shipping firms and
were sold after only a short period of
service.*
2 *The former* Heliopolis *sailed as the*
Royal George *of Canadian Northern
Steamships, known simply as the
Royal Line. For several years she
operated a successful service between
Avonmouth and Montreal.*
3 *Until 1915 the* Cairo *followed a
career identical to that of the*
Heliopolis.

1

2

3

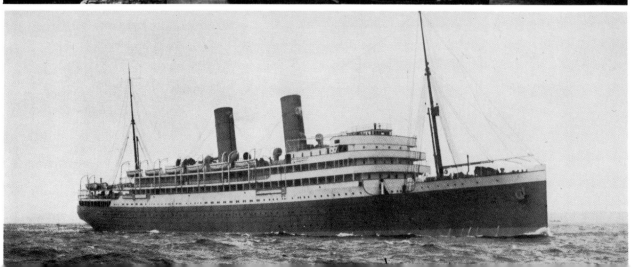

The Tenyo Maru Class of the Toyo Kisen KK

Turbine steamer *Tenyo Maru*
Toyo Kisen KK, Yokohama

Builders: Mitsubishi, Nagasaki
Yard no: 190
13,459 GRT; 175.3 × 18.8 m /
575 × 61.9 ft; Turbines, Parsons;
Triple screw; 20,000 SHP; 18,
max 20.5 kn; Passengers: 275 1st
class, 54 2nd class, 800 3rd class.

1907 Sep 14: Launched.
1908 Apr: Delivered.
Jun 2: Maiden voyage Hong
Kong–San Francisco.
1925 New Parsons turbines fitted.
1926 The Toyo Kisen KK was
taken over by the Nippon Yusen
KK.
1930 Jul 1: Laid up at Nagasaki.
1933 Jun: Sold for breaking-up in
Japan.

Turbine steamer *Chiyo Maru*
Toyo Kisen KK, Yokohama

Builders: Mitsubishi, Nagasaki
Yard no: 191
13,426 GRT; 175.3 × 18.8 m /
575 × 61.9 ft; Turbines, Parsons;
Triple screw; 20,000 SHP; 18,
max 20.5 kn; Passengers: 275 1st
class, 75 2nd class, 800 3rd class.

1907 Dec 7: Launched.
1908 Nov 21: Delivered.
Transpacific service Hong
Kong–San Francisco.
1916 Mar 31: The *Chiyo Maru* ran
aground 20 nautical miles south
of Hong Kong on the island of
Tam Kan, and broke in two a few
days later.

Turbine steamer *Shinyo Maru*
Toyo Kisen KK, Yokohama

Builders: Mitsubishi, Nagasaki
Yard no: 203
13,384 GRT; 175.3 × 18.8 m /
575 × 61.9 ft; Turbines,
Mitsubishi; Triple screw; 20,000
SHP; 18, max 20 kn; Passengers:
210 1st class, 57 2nd class, 754 3rd
class.

1911 Feb 18: Launched.
Aug 15: Delivered. Transpacific
service Hong Kong–San
Francisco.
1926 The Toyo Kisen KK was
taken over by the Nippon Yusen
KK.
1932 Laid up.
1936 Broken up in Japan.

4

1 *The Japanese* Tenyo Maru, *in her time the fastest liner on the Pacific.*
2 *The sister-ship* Chiyo Maru *ran aground in 1916 off Hong Kong.*
3/4 *The third ship of the class, the* Shinyo Maru, *entered service in 1911.*

1

2

3

Four 17,000 Tonners for Hamburg-America and North German Lloyd

Steamship *Prinz Friedrich Wilhelm*
North German Lloyd, Bremen

1921 *Empress of China*;
1921 *Empress of India*;
1922 *Montlaurier*; 1925 *Monteith*;
1925 *Montnairn*

Builders: Tecklenborg, Geestemünde
Yard no: 211
17,082 GRT; 186.8 × 20.8 m / 613 × 68.3 ft; IV exp eng from hull builders; Twin screw; 14,150 IHP; 17, max 19 kn; Passengers: 425 1st class, 338 2nd class, 1,756 3rd class. Crew: 401.

1907 Oct 21: Launched.
1908 May 30: Completed.
Jun 6: Maiden voyage Bremerhaven–New York.
1914 Aug: At the outbreak of war on a cruise to Norway. Sought refuge at Odda.
1916 Broke through to Germany. Ran aground in Danish waters. Laid up at Kiel after a difficult salvage operation.
1919 Mar 30: Handed over to the Shipping Controller, Great Britain. Troop transport under charter to US Navy.
1920 Feb: Liverpool–Quebec service under charter to Canadian Pacific Railway Co, London.
1921 May 13: Bought by Canadian Pacific. Refitted and overhauled in Glasgow. 17,282 GRT.
Aug 2: Renamed *Empress of China*.
Oct 12: Renamed *Empress of India*.
1922 Jun 23: First voyage Liverpool–Quebec.

Dec 13: Renamed *Montlaurier*.
1925 Feb 26: Stranded off Queenstown following rudder damage. Towed to Liverpool and repaired by Cammell Laird.
Apr 15: Badly damaged by fire while in shipyard.
Jun 18: Renamed *Monteith*. Glasgow–Montreal service.
Jul 2: Renamed *Montnairn*.
1927 Antwerp–Quebec service.
1929 Dec 23: Sold for breaking-up.
1930 Broken up in Genoa by SA Co-op Ligure Demolitori Navi.

Steamship *Berlin*
North German Lloyd, Bremen

1921 *Arabic*

Builders: A. G. 'Weser', Bremen
Yard no: 164
17,323 GRT; 186.7 × 21.3 m / 613 × 69.8 ft; IV exp eng, Weser; Twin screw; 16,000 IHP; 17.5, max 19 kn; Passengers: 266 1st class, 246 2nd class, 2,700 3rd class; Crew: 410.

1908 Nov 7: Launched.
1909 Apr 25: Completed.
May 1: Maiden voyage. New York service from Genoa and Bremerhaven.
1914 Sep 18: Auxiliary cruiser with German Navy.
Oct: The *Berlin* laid a minefield between Northern Ireland and Scotland. On Oct 26 the British battleship *Audacious* ran into one of these mines and sank.
Nov 17: The auxiliary cruiser had to enter Drontheim due to shortage of coal and was interned.

1919 Dec 13: Handed over to Shipping Controller. Troop transport under P & O management.
1920 Nov: Sold to White Star Line, Liverpool. Refitted at Portsmouth Dockyard.
1921 Renamed *Arabic*.
Sep 7: First voyage Southampton–New York, then Mediterranean–New York service.
1924 Hamburg–New York service.
1926 Oct 29: First voyage under charter to Red Star Line, Antwerp.
1930 Back to the White Star Line.
1931 Dec: Sold for breaking-up at Genoa

1

2

3

1/2 *The Lloyd steamer* Prinz
Friedrich Wilhelm *(1) was taken over
by Canadian Pacific in 1921. Picture
(2) shows the ship as the* Montlaurier
in 1923.
3 *North German Lloyd's* Berlin *had
to be surrendered to Great Britain in
1919.*

Steamship *Cincinnati*
Hamburg-America Line
Hamburg

1917 *Covington*

Builders: Schichau, Danzig
Yard no: 804
16,339 GRT; 183.9 × 19.9 m /
603 × 63.1 ft; IV exp eng,
Schichau; Twin screw; 11,000
IHP; 15.5, max 16.3 kn;
Passengers: 246 1st class, 332 2nd
class, 448 3rd class, 1,801
steerage; Crew: 385.

1908 Jul 24: Launched.
1909 May 11: Completed.
May 27: Maiden voyage
Hamburg–New York.
1913 May 21: First voyage
Hamburg–Boston.
1914 Aug: Interned in Boston.
1917 Apr 6: Seized. Renamed
Covington, US Navy transport.
1918 Jul 1: Torpedoed by German
submarine U 86 in North Atlantic.
Jul 2: Sank in position 47°24′ N –
07°44′ W.

Steamship *Cleveland*
Hamburg-America Line,
Hamburg

1919 *Mobile*; 1920 *King
Alexander*; 1923 *Cleveland*

Builders: Blohm & Voss,
Hamburg
Yard no: 197
16,960 GRT; 185.0 × 19.9 m /
607 × 63.1 ft; IV exp eng, B & V;
Twin screw; 11,500 IHP; 15.5,
max 16.5 kn; Passengers: 239 1st
class, 224 2nd class, 496 3rd class,
1,882 steerage; Crew: 443.

1908 Sep 26: Launched.
1909 Mar 16: Completed.
Mar 27: Maiden voyage
Hamburg–New York.
1913 Jul 10: First voyage
Hamburg–Boston.
1914 Aug: Laid up in Hamburg
for duration of war.
1919 Mar 26: Handed over to the
Shipping Controller. Taken over
by US Navy as troop transport;
renamed *Mobile*.
1920 Liverpool–New York
service under charter to White
Star Line.
Oct: Sold to Byron SS Co,

London. Renamed *King
Alexander*. Piraeus–New York
service.
1923 To United American Lines,
New York. Renamed *Cleveland*.
Refitted and converted to oil-firing
by Blohm & Voss. 15,746 GRT.
Passengers: 600 cabin class, 1,000
3rd class.
Oct 21: First voyage on
Hamburg–New York service.
The ship was registered under the
Panama flag because of the
American Prohibition laws.
1926 Jul 26: The
Hamburg-America Line bought
back their former ship. German
measurement: 16,971 GRT.
Employed again on
Hamburg–New York service.
1931 Laid up in Hamburg.
1933 Apr 1: To Blohm & Voss for
breaking-up.

4 *The* Berlin *sailed as the* Arabic *for
the White Star Line from 1921.*

4

5 *The Hamburg-America steamer*
Cincinnati *fell victim to a German
submarine in 1918 while serving as a
US transport.*
6 *United American liner* Cleveland.
7 *From 1919 the* Cleveland *sailed
again for Hamburg-America Line for
whom she had been built in 1909.*

Four Ships for CGT

Steamship *Chicago*
CGT, Le Havre

1929 Guadeloupe

Builders: Penhoët, St Nazaire
Yard no: 50
10,471 GRT; 159.6 × 17.6 m /
524 × 57.9 ft; III exp eng,
Penhoët; Twin screw; 9,500 IHP;
16 kn; Passengers: 358 2nd class,
1,250 3rd class.

1907 Nov 5: Launched.
1908 May: Completed.
May 30: Maiden voyage Le
Havre–New York.
1924 Bordeaux–New York.
1928 Refitted for West Indian
service by Chantiers de la
Gironde.
1929 First voyage St
Nazaire–West Indies–Central
America. Renamed *Guadeloupe*.
1936 Oct: Sold for breaking-up at
St Nazaire.

Steamship *Espagne*
CGT, Le Havre

Builders: de Provence, Port de
Bouc
Yard no: 30
11,155 GRT; 171.0 × 18.5 m /
561 × 60.1 ft; IV exp eng from hull
builders; Twin screw; 14,000 IHP;
16.6, max 19.5 kn; Passengers: 296
1st class, 106 2nd class, 86 3rd
class.

1909 Dec 19: Launched.
1910 Sep: Completed.
Oct 5: Maiden voyage St
Nazaire–West Indies–Central
America.
1912 Until 1919 used occasionally
on New York service.
1934 Sold for breaking-up at St
Nazaire.

Steamship *Rochambeau*
CGT, Le Havre

Builders: Penhoët, St Nazaire
Yard no: 56
12,678 GRT; 182.2 × 19.4 m /
598 × 63.1 ft; III exp eng plus
low pressure turbines, from hull
builders; Quadruple screw; 13,700
SHP; 15, max 17.8 kn;
Passengers: 428 2nd class, 200 3rd
class, 1,450 steerage; Crew: 274.

1911 Feb: Launching postponed
because of severe frost.
Mar 2: Launched.
Aug: Completed.
Sep 16: Maiden voyage Le
Havre–New York.
1915 Bordeaux–New York
service.
1918 Le Havre–New York
service again.
1926 Jan: Refitted and
overhauled in La Seyne. Forward
promenade deck glass-enclosed.
Jul: Back in service.
1934 May: Sold for breaking-up to
Gosselin and Dumouries,
Dunkirk.

3

1

2

1 *CGT's* Chicago, *built specially for emigrant service to USA.*
2 *The* Espagne, *which entered service in 1910, sailed on the St Nazaire–Central America route.*
3 *The CGT steamer* Rochambeau.

Turbine steamer *France*
CGT, Le Havre

Laid down as *La Picardie*
1914 *France IV*; 1919 *France*

Builders: Penhoët, St Nazaire
Yard no: 55
23,666 GRT; 217.2 × 23.0 m /
713 × 75.6 ft; Turbines, Penhoët;
Quadruple screw; 45,000 SHP; 23,
max 25 kn; Passengers: 534 1st
class, 442 2nd class, 250 3rd class,
800 steerage; Crew: 500.

1910 Sep 20: Launched.
1912 Apr 3: Completed.
Apr 20: Maiden voyage Le
Havre–New York.
1914 Aug: Auxiliary cruiser;
shortly afterwards troop
transport. Renamed *France IV*.
1916 Served as hospital ship.
1917 Troop transport again after
overhaul in Toulon.
1918 Explosion in engine room. 9
dead. Handed back to CGT.
1919 Jan: Brest–New York
service as *France*; repatriation of
American troops.
Aug: Returned to Le Havre–New
York service.
1923 Refitted and converted to
oil-firing. Passengers: 517 1st
class, 444 2nd class, 510 3rd class,
152 steerage. 23,769 GRT.
1932 Sep: Laid up in Le Havre.
1934 Nov: Sold for breaking-up at
Dunkirk.
1935 Apr 15: Sailed from Le
Havre to Dunkirk.

4/5 *The CGT express steamer* France *(4) served as a hospital ship (5) during the First World War.*

Steamship: *Pericles*
Aberdeen Line, Aberdeen

Builders: Harland & Wolff,
Belfast
Yard no: 392
10,925 GRT; 157.9 × 19.0 m /
518 × 62.3 ft; IV exp eng, H & W;
Twin screw; 6,000 IHP; 14 kn;
Passengers: 100 1st class, 400 3rd
class; Crew: 150.

1907 Dec 21: Launched.
1908 Jun 6: Completed.
Jul 8: Maiden voyage
London–Sydney.
1910 Mar 31: The *Pericles* ran
into a hitherto undetected
underwater reef near Cape
Leeuwin, Australia, and began to
sink. The 300 passengers and crew
took to the boats. The ship sank
bow first two and a half hours
later.

Steamship *Themistocles*
Aberdeen Line, Aberdeen

Builders: Harland & Wolff,
Belfast
Yard no: 412
11,231 GRT; 157.6 × 19.0 m /
517 × 62.3 ft; IV exp eng, H & W;
Twin screw; 6,000 IHP; 14, max
15 kn; Passengers: 103 1st class,
256 3rd class; Crew: 150.

1910 Sep 22: Launched.
1911 Jan 14: Completed.
Feb 16: Maiden voyage
London–Sydney.
1914 Troop transport.
1920 Jul 20: First postwar voyage
London–Australia.
1928 Sep: Liverpool–Sydney–
Brisbane service under White Star
Line management.
1932 Sold to Shaw, Savill &
Albion, Southampton.
Jun 30: First voyage
Liverpool–Brisbane.
1946 Laid up in the River
Blackwater.
1947 Aug 24: Arrived at Dalmuir.
Broken up there by Arnott, Young
& Co.

Steamship *Demosthenes*
Aberdeen Line, Aberdeen

Builders: Harland & Wolff,
Belfast
Yard no: 418
11,233 GRT; 157.6 × 19.0 m /
517 × 62.3 ft; III exp eng, H & W;
plus low pressure turbine, Brown;
Triple screw; 6,000 IHP; 14, max
15 kn; Passengers: 100 1st class,
250 3rd class; Crew: 150.

1911 Feb 28: Launched.
Aug: Completed.
Aug 31: Maiden voyage
London–Sydney.
1915 Troop transport.
1920 Aug 19: First postwar
voyage London–Brisbane.
1929 Feb 2: First voyage
Liverpool–Brisbane under White
Star management.
1931 Oct: Sold for breaking-up to
Hughes, Bolckow & Co.
Scrapped on the Tyne.

1

2

3

4

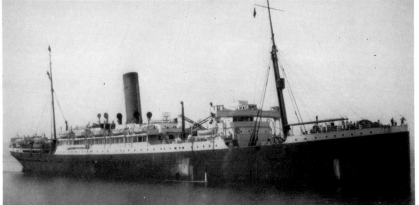

1 *In 1910 Aberdeen Line's* Pericles *ran into an uncharted underwater reef and sank.*
2/3 *The steamship* Themistocles *as an Aberdeen liner (2) and in later years as a Shaw Savill liner (3).*
4 *The* Demosthenes *was broken up in 1931 after 20 years on the Australian service.*

Five British Atlantic Liners

Steamship *Orcoma*
Pacific Steam Nav Co, Liverpool

Builders: Beardmore, Glasgow
Yard no: 492
11,533 GRT; 161.1 × 19.0 m /
530 × 62.2 ft; IV exp eng,
Beardmore; Twin screw; 12,000
IHP; 16, max 17 kn; Passengers:
250 1st class, 200 2nd class, 100 3rd
class, 600 steerage.

1908 Apr 2: Launched.
Aug: Completed.
Aug 27: Maiden voyage, South
America–West Coast.
1915 Apr: Auxiliary cruiser with
the 10th Cruiser Squadron.
1919 Nov 7: First postwar voyage
Liverpool–west coast of South
America.
1923 Refit and modernisation of
passenger accommodation.
Oil-firing.
1933 Jun: Sold for breaking-up to
Hughes, Bolckow & Co; scrapped
at Blyth.

Steamship *Lapland*
Red Star Line, Antwerp

Builders: Harland & Wolff,
Belfast
Yard no: 393
17,540 GRT; 189.0 × 21.4 m /
620 × 70.4 ft; IV exp eng, H & W;
Twin screw; 15,000 IHP; 17 kn;
Passengers: 394 1st class, 352 2nd
class, 1,790 3rd class; Crew: 370.

1908 Jun 27: Launched.
1909 Mar 27: Completed.
Apr: Maiden voyage
Antwerp–New York.
1914 Oct: To White Star Line,
Liverpool.
Oct 29: First voyage
Liverpool–New York.
1917 Jun: Troop transport.
1919 Sep 16: First postwar
voyage Southampton–New York.
18,565 GRT; Passengers: 389 1st
class, 448 2nd class, 1,200 3rd
class.
1920 Taken over by Red Star
Line, Liverpool.
Jan 3: First voyage Antwerp–New
York.
1926 3rd class accommodation
reduced to 540 passengers. Used
mainly for cruising.
1930 Cruising only.
1933 Oct: Sold for breaking-up in
Japan.
1934 Broken up.

Steamship *Laurentic*
White Star Line, Liverpool

Laid down as *Alberta*
Builders: Harland & Wolff,
Belfast
Yard no: 394
14,892 GRT; 172.2 × 20.5 m /
565 × 67.3 ft; III exp eng, H & W,
plus low pressure turbine, Brown;
Triple screw; 11,000 IHP; 16,
max 16.5 kn; Passengers: 230 1st
class, 430 2nd class, 1,000 3rd
class.

1908 Sep 9: Launched. Keel laid
as *Alberta* for Dominion Line,
Liverpool. To White Star Line
before launching.
1909 Apr 15: Delivered.
Apr 29: Maiden voyage
Liverpool–Montreal.
1914 Troop transport.
1917 Jan 25: On a voyage from
Liverpool to Halifax the *Laurentic*
ran into two mines of a field laid by
the German submarine U 80 off
Malin Head, Northern Ireland.
The ship sank very quickly, and
354 of the 475 on board lost their
lives.
The *Laurentic* was carrying a
cargo of gold worth £5 million, the
recovery of which by diving teams
lasted until 1924.

1 *The* Orcoma *of the Pacific Steam
Navigation Co, built in 1908 for the
South America–West Coast service.*
2 *The Red Star liner* Lapland *sailed
until 1914 under the Belgian flag and
following the outbreak of war was
transferred within the Morgan
Combine to the British White Star
Line.*
3 *The White Star steamer* Laurentic,
*which sank in 1917 after hitting two
mines.*

1

2

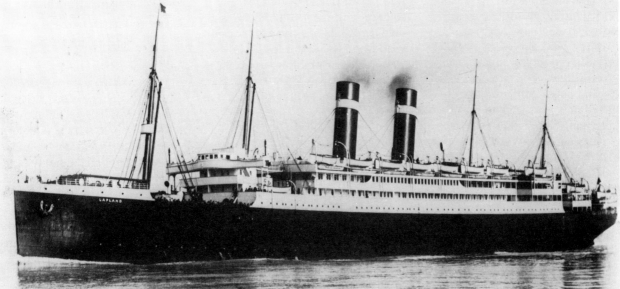

3

Steamship *Megantic*
White Star Line, Liverpool

Builders: Harland & Wolff,
Belfast
Yard no: 399
14,878 GRT; 172.2 × 20.5 m /
565 × 67.3 ft; IV exp eng, H & W;
Twin screw; 11,000 IHP; 16, max
16.5 kn; Passengers: 260 1st class,
430 2nd class, 1,000 3rd class.

1908 Dec 10: Launched. Laid
down for Dominion Line,
Liverpool, as *Albany*. To White
Star Line before launching.
1909 Jun 3: Delivered.
Jun 17: Maiden voyage
Liverpool–Montreal.
1914 Troop transport.
1918 Dec 11: First postwar
voyage Liverpool–New York.
1919 Liverpool–Montreal service
again. Passengers: 325 1st class,
260 2nd class, 550 3rd class.
1920 Jan 9: First voyage
Liverpool–Sydney for British
Government.
1924 Passengers: 452 cabin class,
260 2nd class, 550 3rd class.
1927 One voyage to China as
troop transport.
1928 Mar 22: First voyage
London–Halifax–New York.
Apr 19: London–Montreal
service.
1931 Liverpool–Montreal
service.
Jul: Laid up in Rothesay Bay.
1933 Feb: To Osaka for
breaking-up.

Steamship *Minnewaska*
Atlantic Transport Line, Belfast

Builders: Harland & Wolff,
Belfast
Yard no: 397
14,317 GRT; 187.5 × 19.9 m /
615 × 65.4 ft; IV exp eng, H & W;
Twin screw; 11,000 IHP; 16 kn;
Passengers: 326 1st class.

1908 Nov 12: Launched.
1909 Apr 24: Completed.
May 1: Maiden voyage
London–New York.
1915 Troop transport.
1916 Nov 29: The *Minnewaska*
ran into a floating mine in Suda
Bay near Mudros with 1,800
soldiers on board. The badly
damaged ship was run ashore and
written off as a total loss.
1918 Sold for breaking-up to an
Italian firm.

4

5

4 *Because of the world depression,*
the Megantic, *a sister-ship of the*
Laurentic, *had to be laid up in 1931.*
5 *The* Minnewaska *of the Atlantic*
Transport Line ran into a floating
mine in 1916 with 1,800 soldiers on
board. Fortunately it was possible to
run her ashore, but she had to be
written off as a total loss.

Six Australian Service Steamers of the Orient Line

Steamship *Orsova*
Orient Line, Glasgow

Builders: Brown, Clydebank
Yard no: 383
12,036 GRT; 168.5 × 19.3 m /
553 × 63.3 ft; IV exp eng, Brown;
Twin screw; 14,000 IHP; 18 kn;
Passengers: 268 1st class, 120 2nd
class, 660 3rd class.

1908 Nov 7: Launched.
1909 May 20: Delivered.
Jun 25: Maiden voyage
London–Brisbane.
1915 May: Troop transport.
1917 Mar 14: Badly damaged by
torpedo attack near Eddystone. 6
dead. Run ashore in Cawsand
Bay. Refloated and towed to
Devonport for repairs.
1919 Jan: Seaworthy again; troop
transport to Australia.
Nov 22: First postwar voyage
London–Brisbane.
1933 Refitted as one-class ship;
tourist-class.
1936 Oct: To Bo'ness for
breaking-up.

Steamship *Otway*
Orient Line, Glasgow

Builders: Fairfield, Glasgow
Yard no: 459
12,077 GRT; 168.2 × 19.2 m /
552 × 63.2 ft; IV exp eng,
Fairfield; Twin screw; 14,000
IHP; 18 kn; Passengers: 280 1st
class, 115 2nd class, 700 3rd class.

1908 Nov 21: Launched.
1909 May 29: Delivered.
Jul 9: Maiden voyage
London–Brisbane.
1914 Dec: Auxiliary cruiser with
10th Cruiser Squadron.
1917 Jul 22: Torpedoed and sunk
by German submarine UC 49
north of the Hebrides. 10 dead.

Steamship *Osterley*
Orient Line, Glasgow

Builders: London and Glasgow
Shipbuilding Co, Govan
Yard no: 333
12,129 GRT; 168.5 × 19.3 m /
553 × 63.3 ft; IV exp eng from hull
builders; Twin screw; 14,000 IHP;
18, max 19 kn; Passengers: 270 1st
class, 120 2nd class, 700 3rd class.

1909 Jan 26: Launched.
Jun 22: Delivered.
Aug 6: Maiden voyage
London–Brisbane.
1917 Jun: Troop transport.
1919 Jan: First postwar voyage
London–Brisbane.
1930 Mar: Sold for breaking-up to
P. & W. MacLellan, Glasgow.

1 *The Orient Line had six fast
12,000-ton passenger ships built for its
London–Brisbane service in the years
1908–11. The first of these ships to
enter service was the* Orsova *of 1909.*
2 *The* Otway, *which was sunk by a
submarine in 1917 while serving as
auxiliary cruiser.*
3 *Apart from a period as a troop
transport, the* Osterley *remained on
the Australian service until 1930.*
4 *The steamer* Otranto *was wrecked
in 1918 after colliding with the P & O
liner* Kashmir.

Steamship *Otranto*
Orient Line, Belfast

Builders: Workman, Clark and
Co, Belfast
Yard no: 278
12,124 GRT; 168.8 × 19.5 m /
554 × 64.0 ft; IV exp eng from hull
builders; Twin screw; 14,000 IHP;
18 kn; Passengers: 235 1st class,
186 2nd class, 696 3rd class.

1909 Mar 27: Launched.
Jun 30: Completed.
Oct 1: Maiden voyage
London–Brisbane.
1914 Aug: Auxiliary cruiser.
1918 Oct 6: On a voyage from
New York to Great Britain as
convoy escort and troop
transport, the *Otranto* collided
with the P & O liner *Kashmir* in
the Irish Sea, the Orient liner
being nearly cut in two. The
sinking ship ran aground off Islay.
Although the destroyer *Mounsey*
mounted an immediate rescue
action, 431 lives were lost.

2

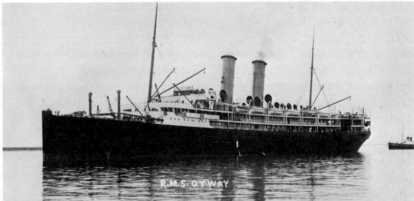

3

4

Steamship *Orvieto*
Orient Line, Belfast

Builders: Workman, Clark & Co,
Belfast
Yard no: 279
12,133 GRT; 168.8 × 19.5 m /
554 × 64.0 ft; IV exp eng from hull
builders; Twin screw; 14,000
IHP; 18 kn; Passengers: 235 1st
class, 185 2nd class, 850 3rd class.

1909 Jul 6: Launched.
Nov: Completed.
Nov 26: Maiden voyage
London–Brisbane.
1914 Troop transport.
1915 Mar: Served as mine-layer.
1916 Jan: Auxiliary cruiser with
10th Cruiser Squadron.
1919 Nov 1: First postwar voyage
London–Brisbane.
1931 Mar: Sold for breaking-up;
scrapped in Great Britain.

Steamship *Orama*
Orient Line, Glasgow

Builders: Brown, Clydebank
Yard no: 403
12,927 GRT; 173.4 × 19.6 m /
569 × 64.2 ft; III exp eng plus
low pressure turbine, Brown;
Triple screw; 14,000 IHP; 18 kn;
Passengers: 240, 1st class, 210
2nd class, 630 3rd class.

1911 Jun 28: Launched.
Oct: Completed.
Nov 10: Maiden voyage
London–Brisbane.
1914 Auxiliary cruiser.
1917 Oct 19: The *Orama* was
torpedoed and sunk by the
German submarine U 62 south of
Ireland while escorting a convoy.

5 *The* Orvieto *made her maiden
voyage in November 1909.*
6 *The* Orama *of 1911 also was a
U-boat victim.*
7 *The* Orama *as an auxiliary cruiser in
World War 1.*

5

6

7

Steamship *Vasari*
Lamport & Holt, Liverpool

1928 *Arctic Queen*;
1935 *Pishchevaya Industriya*

Builders: Raylton Dixon,
Middlesbrough
Yard no: 539
10,117 GRT; 157.4 × 18.1 m /
516 × 59.3 ft; IV exp eng,
Richardson Westgarth & Co;
Single screw; 7,000 IHP; 14 kn;
Passengers: 250 1st class, 130 2nd
class, 200 3rd class.

1908 Dec 8: Launched.
1909 Apr 22: Completed. New
York–La Plata service.
Temporarily registered at 8,401
GRT as shelter-decker.
1919 Jul 24: First voyage
Liverpool–New York under
charter to Cunard.
1921 Again in Lamport & Holt
service.
1928 Sold to Hellyer Bros Ltd,
Hull. Renamed *Arctic Queen*. In
service as cargo-carrier after
removal of passenger
accommodation. 10,078 GRT.
1935 Sold to the Soviet Union.
Renamed *Pishchevaya
Industriya*.
1960 Out of register.

Steamship *Vandyck*
Lamport & Holt, Liverpool

Builders: Workman, Clark & Co,
Belfast
Yard no: 301
10,328 GRT; 155.6 × 18.5 m /
511 × 60.8 ft; IV exp eng from hull
builders; Twin screw; 8,000 IHP;
15 kn; Passengers: 280 1st class,
130 2nd class, 200 3rd class; Crew:
250.

1911 Jun 1: Launched.
Sep 8: Completed. New York–La
Plata service.
1914 Oct 26: On a voyage from
Buenos Aires to New York the
Vandyck was intercepted in the
South Atlantic by the German
cruiser *Karlsruhe*.
Oct 27: After the crew and
passengers of the British steamer
had been put aboard the German
auxiliary vessel *Asuncion*, which
had been ordered to the scene, the
Vandyck was sunk by explosive
charges.

1 *The Lamport & Holt liner* Vasari, *which was sold in 1928 to become a cargo-carrier, latterly under the Soviet flag.*
2 *The* Vandyck, *which entered service in 1911, was sunk in 1914 by the German cruiser* Karlsruhe.
3 *The* Vauban, *sister-ship of the* Vandyck.

Steamship *Vauban*
Lamport & Holt, Liverpool

1913 *Alcala*; 1913 *Vauban*

Builders: Workman, Clark & Co,
Belfast
Yard no: 302
10,660 GRT; 155.6 × 18.5 m /
511 × 60.8 ft; IV exp eng from hull
builders; Twin screw; 8,000 IHP;
15 kn; Passengers: 280 1st class,
130 2nd class, 200 3rd class; Crew:
250.

1912 Jan 20: Launched.
Apr 23: Completed. New
York–La Plata service.
Jun 1: Maiden voyage from
Trieste. Chartered to Royal Mail
Lines for Southampton–La Plata
service.
1913 Apr: Transferred to Royal
Mail Lines, Liverpool. Renamed
Alcala. Back to Lamport & Holt at
end of year; name again *Vauban*.
1919 May 27: First voyage
Liverpool–New York under
Cunard charter.
1922 One voyage under charter
to Royal Mail Lines, then back to
New York–La Plata service.
1930 Laid up at Southampton.

1932 Jan: Sold for breaking-up to
T. W. Ward, Inverkeithing.

Steamship *Vestris*
Lamport & Holt, Liverpool

Builders: Workman, Clark and
Co, Belfast
Yard no: 303
10,494 GRT; 155.6 × 18.5 m /
511 × 60.8 ft; IV exp eng from hull
builders; Twin screw; 8,000 IHP;
15 kn; Passengers: 280 1st class,
130 2nd class, 200 3rd class; Crew:
250.

1912 May 16: Launched.
Sep 3: Completed. New York–La
Plata service.
1919 Mar 8: First voyage
Liverpool–New York under
charter to Cunard.
1922 One voyage under charter to
Royal Mail Lines, then New
York–La Plata service again.
1928 Nov 12: Two days after
leaving New York the *Vestris* ran

into very bad weather in the
Atlantic. The ship developed a
list, which became more
threatening as the result of the
shifting of the cargo and coal in the
bunkers. The *Vestris* sent out an
SOS. Shortly afterwards she
capsized and sank. 112 of the 325
on board were drowned. The
survivors were picked up the next
day from the *Vestris* lifeboats by
the French tanker *Myriam,* the US
battleship *Wyoming,* the US liner
American Shipper and the North
German Lloyd liner *Berlin.*

4

5

6

4 *The* Vauban *sailed as the* Alcala *for Royal Mail Lines for a few months in 1913.*
5 *The* Vestris *sank in a bad storm in the Atlantic in 1928.*
6 *A dramatic picture taken by a cool-headed survivor; confused people try to escape from the sinking* Vestris *down Jacob's ladders into lifeboats.*

Steamship *Ruahine*
New Zealand Line, Plymouth

1949 Auriga

Builders: Denny, Dumbarton
Yard no: 880
10,758 GRT; 151.5 × 18.4 m /
497 × 60.3 ft; III exp eng, Denny;
Twin screw; 5,000 IHP; 14 kn;
Passengers: 56 1st class, 88 2nd
class, 376 3rd class.

1909 Aug 19: Launched.
Nov: Completed.
Nov 25: Maiden voyage
London–Wellington.
1912 Mar 16: Unsuccessful
attempt by the *Ruahine* to tow the
sinking P & O liner *Oceana* into
shallow water after she had been in
collision with the Laeisz sailer
Pisagua in the English Channel.
1920 Converted to oil-firing.
1926 Modernisation and
reduction in passenger
accommodation.
1933 Passengers: 220 tourist
class.
1938 Used only as cargo-carrier.
1949 Sold to Fratelli Grimaldi,
Naples. Renamed *Auriga*.
Passenger accommodation
re-modelled; modernisation of
external appearance. Emigrant
service Naples–South America.
Occasionally used on other
routes; Australian service, Far
East service under charter to
Chargeurs Réunis.
1957 Mar 22: Arrived at Savona
for breaking-up.

Steamship *Rotorua*
New Zealand Line, Plymouth

Builders: Denny, Dumbarton
Yard no: 914
11,130 GRT; 153.0 × 19.0 m /
502 × 62.3 ft; III exp eng plus
low pressure turbine, Denny;
Triple screw; 5,000 IHP; 14 kn;
Passengers: 52 1st class, 72 2nd
class, 410 3rd class.

1910 Jul: Launched.
Oct 5: Completed.
Oct 27: Maiden voyage
London–Wellington.
1917 Mar 22: The *Rotorua* was
torpedoed and sunk 24 nautical
miles east of Start Point by the
German submarine UC 17. One
dead.

Steamship *Remuera*
New Zealand Line, Plymouth

Builders: Denny, Dumbarton
Yard no: 929
11,276 GRT; 153.0 × 19.0 m /
502 × 62.3 ft; III exp eng, Denny;
Twin screw; 5,000 IHP; 14 kn;
Passengers: 60 1st class, 90 2nd
class, 380 3rd class.

1911 Jun 1: Launched.
Sep: Completed.
Sep 28: Maiden voyage
London–Wellington.
1920 Converted to oil-firing.
1933 Modernisation and
reduction of passenger
accommodation; cabin and tourist
class.
1940 Aug 26: Homeward bound
from New Zealand the *Remuera*
was attacked and sunk off Rattray
Head, northeast coast of
Scotland, by German
torpedo-carrying aircraft.

1/2 The New Zealand liner Ruahine
*was sold after 40 years of service to
Fratelli Grimaldi in Naples; she then
sailed for another eight years as the
emigrant carrier* Auriga.

3 The Rotorua *on her maiden voyage
in 1910.*
4 The Remuera *was sunk in 1940 by
German torpedo-carrying aircraft.*

1

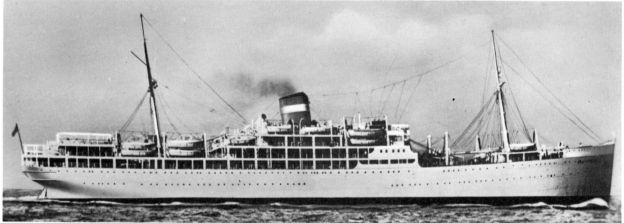

4

Two Union-Castle Express Steamers

Steamship *Balmoral Castle*
Union-Castle Line, London

Builders: Fairfield, Glasgow
Yard no: 468
13,361 GRT; 179.8 × 19.7 m /
590 × 64.5 ft; IV exp eng,
Fairfield; Twin screw; 12,500
IHP; 17 kn; Passengers: 320 1st
class, 220 2nd class, 270 3rd class.

1909 Nov 13: Launched.
1910 Feb: Completed.
Southampton–Cape Town
service. At the end of the year she
sailed to Cape Town under the
White Ensign as a Royal Yacht,
taking members of the British
Royal Family to the opening of the
South African Parliament.
1917 Troop transport.
1919 Southampton–Cape Town
service again. Passenger
accommodation progressively
reduced to 120 1st class, 68 2nd
class, 200 3rd class.
1939 Broken up.

1/2 Balmoral Castle *(1) and*
Edinburgh Castle *(2) were practically
repeats of the 'Saxon' type express
steamers which had entered service
at the turn of the century.*

Steamship *Edinburgh Castle*
Union-Castle Line, London

Builders: Harland & Wolff,
Belfast
Yard no: 410
13,326 GRT; 179.8 × 19.7 m /
590 × 64.5 ft; IV exp eng, H & W;
Twin screw; 12,500 IHP; 17 kn;
Passengers: 320 1st class, 220 2nd
class, 250 3rd class.

1910 Jan 27: Launched.
Apr: Completed.
May: Maiden voyage
Southampton–Cape Town.
1914 Sep 12: Auxiliary cruiser.
Passengers: 235 1st class, 295 2nd
class, 250 3rd class, later reduced
again to 120 1st class, 68 2nd class,
200 3rd class.
1919 Jul: First postwar voyage
Southampton–Cape Town.
1939 Laid up at Southampton.
Aug: Taken over by British
Admiralty. Moved to Freetown as
accommodation ship.
1940 Sold to British Admiralty.
1945 Sep: Sunk by British
warships, 60 nautical miles off
Freetown while being used as
target ship.

Strictly speaking the eight ships dealt with here are not within the compass of this work. The 'tween decks in these ships could, when necessary, be used to take 700–1,000 steerage passengers. They were, however, only seldom used for this purpose. Usually, the ships sailed as cargo-carriers and were classed as shelter-deckers.

Steamship *Rangatira*
Shaw, Savill & Albion, Southampton

Builders: Workman, Clark & Co, Belfast
Yard no: 289
10,118 GRT; 150.6 × 18.6 m / 494 × 61.1 ft; III exp eng from hull builders; Twin screw; 5,600 IHP; 13 kn; Passengers: 1,000 steerage.

1909 Dec 16; Launched.
1910 Feb 7: Completed. Shelter-decker measurement: 7,465 GRT.
Liverpool–Wellington service.
1916 Mar 31: Ashore on Robben Island, Table Bay. Total loss.

Steamship *Pakeha*
Shaw, Savill & Albion, Southampton

1941 *Empire Pakeha*;
1946 *Pakeha*

Builders: Harland & Wolff, Belfast
Yard no: 409
10,481 GRT; 152.4 × 19.2 m / 500 × 63.1 ft; IV exp eng, H & W; Twin screw; 5,600 IHP; 13 kn; Passengers: 1,000 steerage.

1910 May 26: Launched.
Aug 20: Completed. Liverpool–Wellington service.
Shelter-decker measurement: 7,899 GRT.
1939 Sold to British Admiralty. Rebuilt as imitation of HMS *Revenge*.
1941 Handed over to Ministry of War Transport. Again rebuilt, as cargo-carrier. Renamed *Empire Pakeha*. Managed by Shaw, Savill & Albion.
1946 Bought back by Shaw, Savill & Albion. Renamed *Pakeha*.
1950 May: Broken up at Briton Ferry.

Steamship *Zealandic*
White Star Line, Liverpool

1926 *Mamilius*; 1932 *Mamari*

Builders: Harland & Wolff, Belfast
Yard no: 421
10,898 GRT; 152.4 × 19.2 m / 500 × 63.1 ft; IV exp eng, H & W; Twin screw; 5,600 IHP; 13 kn; Passengers: 6 1st class, 1,000 steerage.

1911 Jun 29: Launched.
Oct 12: Delivered.
Oct 30: Maiden voyage Liverpool–Wellington. Measured as shelter-decker: 8,090 GRT.
1926 Jun: Chartered to Aberdeen Line. Renamed *Mamilius*. London–Australia service.
1932 Sold to Shaw, Savill & Albion. Renamed *Mamari*.
1939 Sold to British Admiralty. Rebuilt as imitation of aircraft carrier HMS *Hermes*.
1941 Jun 4: Ashore off Cromer after German air attack. Total loss.

1 The Pakeha *after the Second World War, in the last years of her career.*

1

Steamship *Belgic*
White Star Line, Liverpool

Ex-*Samland*; ex-*Mississippi*;
1913 *Samland*

Builders: New York Shipbuilding
Co, Camden
Yard no: 8
10,151 GRT; 155.4 × 17.7 m /
510 × 58.2 ft; III exp eng from hull
builders; Twin screw; 6,000 IHP;
13, max 14 kn; Passengers: 1,000
steerage.

1902 Dec 15: Launched as
Mississippi for Atlantic Transport
Line, New York.
1903 Apr: Completion. 7,913
GRT. 1,900 steerage passengers.
North Atlantic service.
1906 To Red Star Line, New
York.
Jul 7: First voyage Antwerp–New
York; renamed *Samland*.
1909 Dec: Registered at Antwerp
for Red Star Line.
1910 Jan 1: First voyage
Antwerp–New York.
1911 Apr 7: First voyage
Hamburg–Montreal.
Aug 30: To White Star Line,
Liverpool. Renamed *Belgic*.
10,151 GRT.
Liverpool–Wellington service.
1913 Dec: To Red Star Line,
Antwerp. Renamed *Samland*.
9,748 GRT.
Dec 27: Antwerp–New York
service.
1914 Oct 2: London–New York
service.
1916 Mar 12: New
York–Rotterdam service.
1919 Feb 28: Antwerp–New
York service.
1931 Broken up.

Steamship *Waimana*
Shaw, Savill & Albion,
Southampton

1926 *Herminius*; 1932 *Waimana*;
1941 *Empire Waimana*;
1946 *Waimana*

Builders: Workman, Clark & Co,
Belfast
Yard no: 309
10,389 GRT; 150.6 × 19.2 m /
494 × 63.1 ft; III exp eng from hull
builders; Twin screw; 5,600 IHP;
13 kn; Passengers: 6 1st class,
1,000 steerage.

1911 Sep 12: Launched.
Nov 27: Completed.
Dec 24: Maiden voyage
Liverpool–Wellington.
Shelter-decker measurement,
7,852 GRT.
1926 Chartered to Aberdeen
Line. Renamed *Herminius*. Cargo
service London–Australia.
1932 Back to Shaw, Savill &
Albion as *Waimana*.
1939 Sold to British Admiralty.
Rebuilt as imitation of battleship
HMS *Resolution*.
1941 Jul: Handed over to
Ministry of War Transport.
Rebuilt again as cargo-carrier.
Renamed *Empire Waimana*.
Managed by Shaw, Savill &
Albion.
1946 Bought back by Shaw, Savill
& Albion. Renamed *Waimana*.
1952 Jan: To Milford Haven for
breaking-up.

2

3

2 *White Star Liner* Zealandic.
Pictured here as the Mamilius *under charter to the Aberdeen Line.*
3 *Like the other emigrant ships covered in this section, the* Waimana *was used mainly as a cargo vessel.*

Steamship *Indrapura*
Indra Line (T. B. Royden),
Liverpool

1916 Port Adelaide

Builders: Swan, Hunter &
Wigham Richardson, Newcastle
Yard no: 887
10,286 GRT; 154.9 × 18.7 m /
508 × 61.3 ft; III exp eng,
Wallsend Slipway; Twin screw;
5,400 IHP; 13, max 15 kn;
Passengers: 12 1st class, 800
steerage.

1911 Oct 10: Launched.
Dec: Completed.
London–Sydney service.
Shelter-decker measurement:
8,144 GRT.
1914 To Commonwealth and
Dominion Line, London.
Continued in Australia service.
1916 Renamed *Port Adelaide*.
1917 Feb 3: Torpedoed and sunk
180 nautical miles southwest of
Fastnet by German submarine
U 81.

Steamship *Hawkes Bay*
Tyser Line, London

1916 Port Napier; *1936 Martand*;
1938 Martano; *1938 Mar Bianco*

Builders: Workman, Clark & Co,
Belfast
Yard no: 313
10,641 GRT; 154.9 × 18.7 m /
508 × 61.3 ft; III exp eng from hull
builders; Twin screw; 5,400 IHP;
13 kn; Passengers: 750 steerage.

1912 Sep 27: Launched.
Dec 18: Delivered.
1913 Jan: Maiden voyage
London–Sydney. Shelter-decker
measurement: 8,491 GRT.
1914 To Commonwealth and
Dominion Line, London.
Continued in Australia service.
1916 Renamed *Port Napier*.
1936 To T. & J. Brocklebank,
Liverpool; renamed *Martand*.
1938 To A. Zanchi, Genoa;
renamed *Martano* and then again
in the same year, *Mar Bianco*.
1943 Sep: Taken over by German
Navy after the Italian
capitulation.
Dec 7: Sunk by Allied bombers in
Zara (Zadar, Yugoslavia).

Steamship *Makarini*
Tyser Line, London

1914 Port Nicholson

Builders: Workman, Clark & Co,
Belfast
Yard no: 310
10,624 GRT; 154.9 × 18.7 m /
508 × 61.4 ft; III exp eng from hull
builders; Twin screw; 5,400 IHP;
13, max 14.5 kn; Passengers: 750
steerage.

1912 Feb 3: Launched.
Apr: Completed.
London–Sydney service.
1914 To Commonwealth &
Dominion Line, London.
Renamed *Port Nicholson*.
Continued in Australian service.
1917 Jan 15: 15 nautical miles
west of Dunkirk the *Port
Nicholson* sank after hitting a mine
laid by the German submarine
UC 1.

4/5 The steamships Indrapura,
Makarini *(4) and* Hawkes Bay *(5)
sailed in the Tyser Line's Australian
service before being taken over by the
Commonwealth and Dominion Line
(now the Port Line) in 1914.*

5

172 The Cunard Liners Franconia and Laconia

Steamship *Franconia*
Cunard Line, Liverpool

Builders: Swan, Hunter &
Wigham Richardson, Newcastle
Yard no: 857
18,150 GRT; 190.5 × 21.7 m /
625 × 71.3 ft; IV exp eng,
Wallsend; 18,000 IHP; 17, max 18
kn; Passengers; 300 1st class, 350
2nd class, 2,200 3rd class.

1910 Jul 23: Launched.
1911 Jan 23: Completed.
Feb 25: Maiden voyage
Liverpool–New York, then
Liverpool–Boston service and
cruising.
1915 Feb: Troop transport.
1916 Oct 4: The *Franconia* was
torpedoed 195 nautical miles
southeast of Malta by the German
submarine UB 47, and sank 50
minutes later. 12 dead.

Steamship *Laconia*
Cunard Line, Liverpool

Builders: Swan, Hunter &
Wigham Richardson, Newcastle
Yard no: 877
18,099 GRT; 190.5 × 21.7 m /
625 × 71.3 ft; IV exp eng from hull
builders; Twin screw; 18,000 IHP;
17, max 18 kn; Passengers: 300 1st
class, 350 2nd class, 2,200 3rd
class.

1911 Jul 27: Launched.
Dec 10: Completed.
1912 Jan 20: Maiden voyage
Liverpool–New York; then
Liverpool–Boston service.
1914 Oct: Auxiliary cruiser.
1916 Sep 9: North Atlantic
service again for Cunard Line.
1917 Feb 25: The *Laconia* was
torpedoed and sunk 160 nautical
miles northwest of Fastnet by the
German submarine U 50. 12 dead.

1/2 *The sister-ships* Franconia *(1) and*
Laconia *(2), built for Cunard Line's
Canadian service, fell victims to
German submarines in the First World
War.*

1

2

Blue Funnel Liners

Steamship *Aeneas*
Blue Funnel Line, Liverpool

Builders: Workman, Clark & Co, Belfast
Yard no: 294
10,049 GRT; 155.1 × 18.4 m / 509 × 60.4 ft; III exp eng from hull builders; Twin screw; 5,700 IHP; 14 kn; Passengers: 288 1st class.

1910 Aug 23: Launched.
Nov 1: Completed.
Nov 18: Maiden voyage Glasgow–Brisbane.
1914 Troop transport.
1920 May 29: First postwar voyage Glasgow–Brisbane.
1925 Entered Blue Funnel Line's Far East service.
1940 Jul 2: The *Aeneas* sailing in convoy was bombed and sunk by German aircraft 21 nautical miles southeast of Start point. 19 dead.

Steamship *Ascanius*
Blue Funnel Line, Liverpool

1949 *San Giovannino*

Builders: Workman, Clark and Co, Belfast
Yard no: 295
10,048 GRT; 155.1 × 18.4 m / 509 × 60.4 ft; III exp eng from hull builders; Twin screw; 5,700 IHP; 14 kn; Passengers: 288 1st class.

1910 Oct 29: Launched.
Dec 21: Completed.
Dec 30: Maiden voyage Glasgow–Brisbane.
1914 Aug: Troop transport.
1920 Aug 21: First postwar voyage Glasgow–Brisbane.
1926 Passengers: 180 1st class.
1945 Marseilles–Haifa service.
1949 Sold to Cia de Nav Florencia SA, Panama. Renamed

San Giovannino. Did not enter service; laid up at La Spezia.
1953 Mar: Sold for breaking-up at La Spezia.

Steamship *Anchises*
Blue Funnel Line, Liverpool

Builders: Workman, Clark & Co, Belfast
Yard no: 296
10,046 GRT; 155.1 × 18.4 m / 509 × 60.4 ft; III exp eng from hull builders; Twin screw; 5,700 IHP; 14 kn; Passengers: 288 1st class.

1911 Jan 12: Launched.
Mar 10: Completed.
Glasgow–Brisbane service.
1914 Troop transport.
1922 Sep: First postwar voyage Glasgow–Brisbane.

2

1926 Passengers 180 1st class.
1941 Feb 27: Badly damaged in
German air attack.
Feb 28: In repeated air attacks the
Anchises was sunk off the
northwest coast of Ireland by an
aerial bomb. 12 dead.

1

1-3 *The sister-ships* Aeneas *(1)*
Ascanius *(2) and* Anchises *(3) for the*
Blue Funnel Line's
Glasgow–Brisbane service.

3

Steamship *Talthybius*
Blue Funnel Line, Liverpool

1942 *Taruyasu Maru*;
1947 *Empire Evenlode*

Builders: Scott's, Greenock
Yard no: 436
10,224 GRT; 157.9 × 18.4 m /
518 × 60.4 ft; III exp eng, Scott's;
Twin screw; 5,700 IHP; 13.5 kn;
Passengers: 600 steerage.

1911 Nov 7: Launched.
1912 Completed. Liverpool–Far
East service.
1942 Feb 6: Sunk in Singapore.
Raised by the Japanese. Renamed
Taruyasu Maru.
1945 Jun 30: Struck mine off Sado
and sank.
1947 Raised by British. Repaired
at Hong Kong and renamed
Empire Evenlode.
1949 Sep 7: Arrived at Briton
Ferry for breaking-up.

Steamship *Ixion*
Blue Funnel Line, Liverpool

Builders: Scott's, Greenock
Yard no: 442
10,221 GRT; 157.9 × 18.4 m /
518 × 60.4 ft; III exp eng, Scott's;
Twin screw; 5,700 IHP; 13.5 kn;
Passengers 600 steerage.

1912 Oct 29: Launched.
Dec: Completed.
Liverpool–Far East service.
1941 May 7: While sailing in
convoy 200 nautical miles south of
Reykjavik, the *Ixion* was
torpedoed and sunk by German
submarine U 94 in position
61°29′ N – 22°40′ W.

Steamship *Nestor*
Blue Funnel Line, Liverpool

Builders: Workman, Clark & Co,
Belfast
Yard no: 318
14,501 GRT; 176.8 × 20.8 m /
580 × 68.4 ft; III exp eng from hull
builders; Twin screw; 7,750 IHP;
14 kn; Passengers: 350 1st class.

1912 Dec 7: Launched.
1913 Apr: Completed.
May 19: Maiden voyage
Liverpool–Brisbane.
1915 Sep: Troop transport.
1920 Apr 22: First postwar
voyage Glasgow–Brisbane.
1926 Passengers: 250 1st class.
1935 Passengers: 175 1st class.
Increased again to 250 during
Second World War.
1950 Jul 2: From Liverpool to
Faslane; there broken-up by
British Iron and Steel Corp.

4/5 *The steamships* Talthybius *(4)
and* Ixion *(5), built for the Far East
service, had accommodation for 600
steerage passengers.*
6 *With her 14,501 GRT the* Nestor
*was at the time of her entering service
the largest liner on the Australian
route.*

4

5

6

Steamship *Ulysses*
Blue Funnel Line, Liverpool

Builders: Workman, Clark & Co,
Belfast
Yard no: 319
14,499 GRT; 176.8 × 20.8 m /
580 × 68.4 ft; III exp eng from hull
builders; Twin screw; 7,750 IHP;
14 kn; Passengers: 350 1st class.

1913 Jul 5: Launched.
Oct 22: Completed.
Glasgow/Liverpool–Brisbane
service.
1915 Troop transport.
1920 Sep: First postwar voyage
Glasgow–Brisbane.
1926 Passengers: 250 1st class.
1935 Passengers: 175 1st class,
increased to 250 during Second
World War.

1942 Apr 11: The *Ulysses* was
torpedoed and sunk by German
submarine U 160 off Palm Beach,
position 34°23′ N – 75°5′ W.

7/8 *Blue Funnel liner* Ulysses,
sister-ship to the Nestor.

Steamship *Olympic*
White Star Line, Liverpool

Builders: Harland & Wolff,
Belfast
Yard no: 400
45,324 GRT; 268.8 × 28.2 m /
882 × 92.5 ft; III exp eng plus
low pressure turbine, H & W;
Triple screw; 51,000 IHP; 21,
max 22 kn; Passengers: 1,054 1st
class, 510 2nd class, 1,020 3rd
class; Crew: 860.

1910 Oct 20: Launched.
1911 May 31: Completed.
Jun 14: Maiden voyage
Southampton–New York. Biggest
ship in the world until 1912/13.
Sep 20: The *Olympic* collided with
the British cruiser *Hawke* off
Southampton. Both ships badly
damaged.
1912 Rebuilt by Harland & Wolff
during winter months 1912/13.
Safety measures (bulkheads)
improved in the light of the *Titanic*
disaster. Additional lifeboats
installed. Passenger
accommodation now for 735 1st
class, 675 2nd class, 1,030 3rd
class. 46,439 GRT.
1914 Oct: Unsuccessful attempt
by *Olympic* to tow the British
battleship *Audacious*, sinking
after striking a mine in the Irish
Sea. After the *Olympic* had taken
on board the battleship's
complement and connected
towing lines, the *Audacious* sank.
1915 Sep: Troop transport.
1917 Apr 4: The *Olympic* became
a troop transport under the White
Ensign.
1918 May 12: The *Olympic* was
attacked in the Atlantic by the
German submarine U 103. The
liner was able to avoid the

torpedoes, whereby the
submarine ran under the bows of
the *Olympic,* was badly damaged
and sank. One crew member was
rescued by a US destroyer.
1919 Aug 12: To Belfast for
overhaul. Converted to oil-firing.
Passengers: 750 1st class, 500 2nd
class, 1,150 3rd class.
1920 Jul 21: First postwar voyage
Southampton–New York.
1928 Passengers: 675 1st class,
561 tourist class, 819 3rd class.
Reduced again at the beginning of
the 'thirties to 618 1st class, 447
tourist class and 382 3rd class.
1934 Feb: The White Star Line
merged with the Cunard Line to
form Cunard-White Star Line.
May 16: In thick fog *Olympic*
rammed the Nantucket.lightship

which at once sank. 7 dead.
1935 Apr 12: Laid up at
Southampton.
Sep: Sold to Metal Industries for
breaking-up.
Oct 13: Arrived in Jarrow, where
she was partially dismantled.
1937 Sep 19: What was left of her
hull was towed to Inverkeithing
and scrapped there.

1 *The launch of the* Olympic.

1

Steamship *Titanic*
White Star Line, Liverpool

Builders: Harland & Wolff, Belfast
Yard no: 401
46,329 GRT; 269.1 × 28.2 m / 883 × 92.5 ft; III exp eng plus low pressure turbine, H & W; Triple screw; 51,000 IHP; 21, max 22 kn; Passengers: 905 1st class, 564 2nd class, 1,134 3rd class; Crew: 900.

1911 May 31: Launched.
1912 Apr 2: Delivered. Largest ship in the world at this time.
Apr 10: Maiden voyage Southampton–New York.

Apr 14: The *Titanic* approached the Grand Banks. She was sailing on the steamer route in the south of the North Atlantic, internationally agreed for the avoidance of danger from ice and fog.
9.00 hrs: Ice-warning from Cunard liner *Caronia*.
13.42 hrs: Ice-warning from White Star liner *Baltic*.
13.55 hrs: Ice-warning from Hamburg-America liner *Amerika*.
19.30 hrs: Ice-warning from Leyland steamer *Californian*.
21.40 hrs: Ice-warning from ATL steamer *Mesaba*.
All these warnings applied to the same ice-field and were

all received by the *Titanic* which nevertheless continued to sail westwards at her full service speed of a good 21 knots. On a clear night, with good visibility, this was and still is today internationally acceptable and in order. The look-outs, two as usual, were in the crow's nest.

The radio was somewhat overloaded because of the many ice-warnings and passengers' numerous private messages.
23.00 hrs: The *Californian* called the *Titanic* directly. She reported that she was lying in drifting ice and that . . . Before she could give her position, she was rather brusquely told by the *Titanic's*

2

3

29

4

2 *The White Star liners* Titanic *and* Olympic *on the stocks at Harland & Wolff.*
3/4 *The* Olympic, *the world's first 40,000 tonner. Both photos show the ship after the 1912/13 provision of increased life-saving and safety equipment.*
5 *The* Titanic *during fitting-out in dry dock at Harland & Wolff.*

radio-operator to keep off the wavelength and not to disturb the wireless traffic. At this moment, the *Californian* was about 25 nautical miles to the north of the *Titanic*.

23.40 hrs: Look-out reported iceberg 1,600 ft ahead. The First Officer ordered 'Rudder hard to port' followed by 'All engines full astern'; commands which any other seaman also would have given in this situation. Only after the manoeuvre had gone wrong by a few critical feet and the *Titanic* suffered her fatal injury, was it clear that in this particular circumstance, possibly the most suitable order would have been merely 'full astern' — and then to coast straight into the iceberg. Possibly the *Titanic* would then have remained afloat. She would have suffered a badly deformed bow and other damage. There could have been a few deaths, and injuries amongst the survivors. This is, of course, only a theory. All one can say with certainty is that neither public nor experts were prepared for such a disaster.

If there had been a chance of avoiding the iceberg completely the action taken would have been reasonable, and had the *Titanic* been equipped with a modern balanced rudder (as was, for instance, the *Mauretania* of 1907) the manoeuvre employed might have been successful.

But it was not successful. The iceberg cut a 300-foot gash in her starboard side from the bow to the forward boiler room. Five compartments were flooded. It is hardly likely that even modern sub-division, let alone the *Titanic's* by present-day standards quite antiquated watertight arrangements, would have coped with the inrush resulting from such a fracture. With the former, however, she might perhaps have remained afloat a decisive three hours longer.

Apr 15: 00.05 hrs: It was realised on the bridge that the liner was sinking. The order was given to prepare lifeboats and the passengers were roused.

00.15 hrs: The first distress call went out. The North German Lloyd liner *Frankfurt*, the Canadian Pacific *Mount Temple*, the Allan liner *Virginian*, the Russian *Birma* and the *Olympic* all replied. The Cunard liner *Carpathia* was nearest to the *Titanic*, 60 nautical miles away, and proceeded at full speed, arriving at the scene of the disaster four hours later. There was, in fact another ship even closer. Just 10 miles away and visible, lay the *Californian*, 6,223 GRT. She had not received the distress call. Her radio operator had gone to bed an hour earlier, after the *Titanic* had 'thrown him off the wavelength'. The stationary four-funnelled liner was in fact seen from the *Californian*, without anyone knowing she was the *Titanic*. It was assumed that she was lying stopped for the night, like the *Californian*, because of the ice. Attempts at making contact with morse-lamps were unsuccessful. The *Titanic's* distress rockets were later seen by the *Californian*, but were not recognised as such, because they were white. In an emergency at sea, distress rockets are customarily blue or red. The morse-lamps were tried again, but received no answer and were given up. When the *Titanic* was no longer to be seen it was assumed that she had continued on her course. Only the next morning did the captain of the *Californian* learn that he could have rescued 1,500 people the previous night. It remains incomprehensible why nobody saw the *Californian* from the *Titanic*.

00.25 hrs: The first lifeboat was lowered, followed by the second and the third. Instead of 240, there were only 63 people in the three boats. Still the passengers would not stir themselves to leave the seemingly safe ship. There were 2,206 people aboard the *Titanic* on this voyage. Had she been fully-booked there would have been 3,350, yet there was room only for 1,178 people in the 20 lifeboats. This disparity between passenger numbers and lifeboat capacity was, at that time, quite normal among shipping lines and no contravention of legal requirements. It is still difficult to understand, however, why in these circumstances the first boats lowered were only 20 per cent full.

The rapidly dipping fore part of the ship was making clear to those up till now still optimistic passengers the seriousness of the situation. The next lifeboats launched were therefore nearly fully occupied. The bulkhead

6

6 *The* Titanic *on her initial crossing from Belfast to Southampton.*
7 *White Star liner* Titanic. *The sinking of the ship is, to this day, the worst-ever shipping disaster (excluding wartime sinkings) and led to far reaching alterations in international regulations for safety at sea.*

7

between boiler rooms 5 and 6 collapsed. The forward section was by this time completely under water.

01.40 hrs: The last distress rockets were fired.

02.05 hrs: The last boat was lowered into the water. Well over 1,500 people were still on board.

02.10 hrs: Last wireless message. The steamer was sinking bow first, propellers high out of the water.

02.15 hrs: The *Titanic* was now standing nearly perpendicular on her bow and began to sink more rapidly.

02.18 hrs: The lights went out. The engines broke loose from their mountings.

02.20 hrs: The *Titanic* went down in position 41°46′ N — 50°14′ W.

04.10 hrs: The *Carpathia* arrived. The Cunard liner had forced the most out of her boilers and engines. She was able to take on 703 survivors. For 1,503 people there was no rescue.

The following table is interesting; it was published by the British periodical *The Shipbuilder* in the summer of 1912. The percentages of rescued were as follows:

	Total on board	Total rescued	Percentage rescued
1st class passengers			
Men	173	58	34
Women	144	139	97
Children	5	5	100
Total	322	202	63
2nd class passengers			
Men	160	13	8
Women	93	78	84
Children	24	24	100
Total	277	115	42
3rd class passengers			
Men	454	55	12
Women	179	98	55
Children	76	23	30
Total	709	176	23
Total passengers	1308	493	38
Crew	898	210	23
Total people on board	2206	703	32

This was according to *The Shipbuilder*. One should add, that the total of rescued crew members corresponds to the crew total necessary to handle the lifeboats.

Steamship *Britannic*
White Star Line, Liverpool

Builders: Harland & Wolff, Belfast
Yard no: 433
48,158 GRT; 275.2 × 28.7 m / 903 × 94.0 ft; III exp eng plus low pressure turbine, H & W; Triple screw; 60,000 IHP; 21 kn; Passengers: 790 1st class, 830 2nd class, 953 3rd class; Crew: 950.

1914 Feb 26: Launched.
1915 Nov 13: The British Admiralty ordered the completion of the *Britannic* as a hospital ship. Dec 8: Trials.
Dec 12: Delivered and commissioned as hospital ship.
1916 Nov 21: The *Britannic* ran into a minefield laid by the German submarine U 73 in the Aegean, four nautical miles west of Port St Nikolo, and struck a mine. The resultant explosion was on the starboard side near the bulkhead between compartments 2 and 3. For some reason unexplained, the watertight door system in the forward part of the ship failed to function. Water flowed unchecked into five compartments including the two forward boiler rooms. The *Britannic* sent out an SOS. Her master ordered course for the coast in order to run his ship ashore. Meanwhile a start was made on getting the 1,134 people on board into the lifeboats. Two lifeboats were shattered by the

thrashing propellers which were now protruding from the water. One hour after the explosion the *Britannic* heeled over to starboard and sank. 21 people (28 according to other sources) lost their lives, most of them in the two destroyed lifeboats. Shortly afterwards the survivors were picked up by the British cruiser *Heroic,* the destroyers *Foxhound* and *Scourge,* and a French tug.

8 *This painting from a shipping line brochure in 1914 shows the* Britannic *as she would have looked as a White Star liner.*
9 *The third ship of the class, the* Britannic, *was completed as a hospital ship in 1915 and sank in 1916 after striking a mine.*

9

The Argyllshire-Class

Steamship *Argyllshire*
Scottish Shire Line Ltd, Glasgow

1933 Clan Urquhart

Builders: Brown, Clydebank
Yard no: 399
10,392 GRT; 165.8 × 18.7 m /
544 × 61.4 ft; IV exp eng, Brown;
Twin screw; 6,500 IHP; 13.5, max
14.5 kn; Passengers: 130 1st class.

1911 Feb 27: Launched.
Jul: Completed.
Aug 5: Maiden voyage
London–Brisbane.
1912 Passengers: 66 1st class.
1914 Troop transport.
1920 Back on New Zealand
service. Passengers: 133 1st class,
76 3rd class.
1929 Laid up in the Gareloch.
1932 Nov: To Clan Line
Steamers, Glasgow. Refitted and
overhauled by Brown,
Clydebank. Passenger
accommodation removed. 9,564
GRT.
1933 Renamed *Clan Urquhart*.
Service to South and East Africa.
1936 Broken up by T. W. Ward at
Briton Ferry.

Steamship *Shropshire*
Federal SN Co, London

1922 Rotorua

Builders: Brown, Clydebank
Yard no: 400
11,911 GRT; 165.8 × 18.7 m /
544 × 61.4 ft; IV exp eng, Brown;
Twin screw; 6,500 IHP; 13.5, max
14.5 kn; Passengers: 130 1st class.

1911 Apr 27: Launched.
Sep: Completed.
Oct 28: Maiden voyage
Liverpool-Brisbane.
1912 Passengers: 66 1st class.
1914 Aug: Troop transport.
1917 Back to Australian service.
1921 Oct 28: Badly damaged by
fire.
Nov 11: Laid up in Falmouth after
further fire-damage.
1922 To New Zealand Line,
London, but remained registered
under ownership of Federal SN
Co. Converted to oil-firing.
Passengers: 131 1st class, 270 2nd
class. 270 3rd class, 12,184 GRT.
Renamed *Rotorua*.
1923 Mar 29: First voyage

Southampton–Wellington.
1932 Tourist class only. 10,890
GRT.
1940 Dec 11: The *Rotorua* was
torpedoed and sunk 110 nautical
miles west of St Kilda, Scotland,
by the German submarine U 96.
20 dead.

1 *The* Argyllshire *camouflaged
during the First World War.*

2

3

4

2 *Scottish Shire liner* Argyllshire, *built for the Australian service shared with the Federal Line.*
3/4 *The Federal Line's* Shropshire *(3) was handed over to the New Zealand Line as the* Rotorua *(4) in 1922.*

Steamship *Wiltshire*
Federal SN Co, London

Builders: Brown, Clydebank
Yard no: 401
10,390 GRT; 165.8 × 18.7 m /
544 × 61.4 ft; IV exp eng, Brown;
Twin screw; 6,500 IHP; 13.5, max
14.5 kn; Passengers: 131 1st class,
reduced to 66 1st class after one
voyage.

1911 Dec 19: Launched.
1912 Feb 15: Completed.
Mar 16: Maiden voyage
Liverpool–Brisbane.
1914 Troop transport. Back to
Australian service after the war.
1922 May 31: While approaching
Auckland the *Wiltshire* ran
aground in stormy weather in
Rosalie Bay near Great Barrier
Island. She broke in two the next
day.

5/6 *The last ship of the class, the* Wiltshire, *ran aground off Auckland in 1922.*

Steamship *Paul Lecat*
Messageries Maritimes, Marseille

Builders: Constructions Navales,
La Ciotat
Yard no: 136
12,989 GRT; 161.0 × 18.7 m /
529 × 58.3 ft; IV exp eng from hull
builders; Twin screw; 11,000 IHP;
15, max 16.5 kn; Passengers: 194
1st class, 145 2nd class, 109 3rd
class, 826 steerage; Crew: 350.

1911 Mar 19: Launched.
Sep 9: Completed.
Sep 22: Maiden voyage
Marseille–Far East. At the
planning stage, the ship had been
intended to be named *Buenos
Ayres* for the South America
service.
1915 Troop transport.
1918 Back to Marseille–Far East
service.
1928 Dec 30: The *Paul Lecat*
caught fire in Marseille harbour.
She blazed until the next day and
was completely burned out.
1929 Jan 3: Declared a total loss.
Jun: Sold for breaking-up at La
Spezia.

1 *The* Paul Lecat *at her builders'
fitting-out berth.*
2 *In December, 1928, the* Paul Lecat
was totally destroyed by fire.

Steamship *André Lebon*
Messageries Maritimes,
Marseille

Builders: Constructions Navales,
La Ciotat
Yard no: 142
13,682 GRT; 159.4 × 18.7 m /
523 × 58.3 ft; IV exp eng from hull
builders; Twin screw; 11,000 IHP;
15, max 16.5 kn; Passengers: 199
1st class, 182 2nd class, 140 3rd
class; Crew: 350.

1913 Oct 27: Launched.
1915 Dec: Completed.
Dec 26: First voyage
Marseille–North Africa, as troop
transport.
1916 Hospital ship.
1919 Marseille–Far East service
after refitting as passenger ship.

1923 Sep 1: Stationed for 14 days
at Yokohama to assist after Tokyo
earthquake disaster.
1944 Mar 1: Badly damaged in
Toulon by allied air attack. Sunk
by the Germans during their
withdrawal.
1945 May 1: Raised. Repaired at
Marseille. Passengers: 287 1st
class, 171 2nd class, 107 3rd class.
1946 Oct 19: First postwar
voyage Marseille–Far East.
1952 Dec: Sold for breaking-up at
La Seyne.

3 *Steamship* André Lebon *of
Messageries Maritimes.*

3

Steamship *Cameronia*
Anchor Line, Glasgow

Builders: Henderson, Glasgow
Yard no: 472
10,963 GRT; 162.1 × 19.0 m /
532 × 62.2 ft; III exp eng,
Henderson; Twin screw; 10,000
IHP; 16 kn; Passengers: 250 1st
class, 450 2nd class, 1,000 3rd
class.

1911 May 27: Launched.
Sep: Completed.
Sep 13: Maiden voyage
Glasgow–New York.
1915 Employed on joint service
with Cunard,
Glasgow–Liverpool–New York.
1917 Jan: Troop transport.
Apr 15: The *Cameronia* was
torpedoed and sunk 150 nautical
miles east of Malta by the German
submarine U 33. 210 dead.

1 *The* Cameronia, *built for the Glasgow–New York service.*

Hamburg-South America Liner Cap Finisterre

Steamship *Cap Finisterre*
Hamburg-South America Line,
Hamburg

1921 *Taiyo Maru*

Builders: Blohm & Voss,
Hamburg
Yard no: 208
14,503 GRT; 180.0 × 19.9 m /
591 × 65.3 ft; IV exp eng, B & V;
Twin screw; 10,600 IHP; 16.5 kn;
Passengers: 297 1st class, 222 2nd
class, 870 3rd class. Crew: 300.

1911 Aug 8: Launched.
Nov 18: Completed.
Dec 2: Maiden voyage
Hamburg–La Plata ports.
1914 Aug: Laid up in Hamburg
for duration of war.
1919 Apr 4: Surrendered to USA.
US Navy transport. Handed over
to Great Britain at the end of the
year. Managed for the Shipping
Controller by the Orient Line.
1920 Jul: To Japan as reparations.
1921 To Toyo Kisen KK, Tokyo.
Renamed *Taiyo Maru*. 14,457
GRT; Yokohama–San Francisco
service.
1926 Toyo Kisen KK taken over
by Nippon Yusen KK.
1934 Refitted and modernised.
New boilers. 19 kn.
1941 Dec: The *Taiyo Maru*
reconnoitred the route which the
Japanese attacking force was to
take towards Pearl Harbour
shortly afterwards.
1942 May 8: The *Taiyo Maru* was
torpedoed and sunk southwest of
Kyushu in the Pacific by the
American submarine *Grenadier*.

1 *The* Cap Finisterre *in her early years, still with the yellow Hamburg-South America funnel.*
2 *Nippon Yusen Kaisha liner* Taiyo Maru, *the former* Cap Finisterre.

The B-Class of the P & O Line

Steamship *Ballarat*
P & O Line, Greenock

Builders: Caird, Greenock
Yard no: 318
11;120 GRT; 157.0 × 19.0 m /
515 × 62.8 ft; IV exp eng, Caird;
Twin screw; 9,000 IHP; 14, max
15 kn; Passengers: 1,100 3rd class.

1911 Sep 23: Launched.
Nov: Completed.
London–Sydney service.
1914 Troop transport.
1917 Apr 25: Torpedoed by
German submarine UB 32 24
nautical miles southwest of Wolf
Rock in the English Channel.
Apr 26: The *Ballarat* sank, after all
1,752 on board had been able to
leave the ship.

Steamship *Beltana*
P & O Line, Greenock

Builders: Caird, Greenock
Yard no: 319
11,120 GRT; 157.0 × 19.0 m /
515 × 62.8 ft; IV exp eng, Caird;
Twin screw; 9,000 IHP; 14, max
15 kn; Passengers: 1,100 3rd class.

1912 Jan 24: Launched.
May: Completed.
London–Sydney service.
1914 Troop transport.
1919 London–Sydney service
again.
1930 Sold to Toyo Hogei KK,
Osaka. Plans for rebuilding her as
a whaler, but these were not
realised.
1933 Broken up in Japan.

Steamship *Benalla*
P & O Line, Greenock

Builders: Caird, Greenock
Yard no: 322
11,118 GRT; 157.0 × 19.0 m /
515 × 62.8 ft; IV exp eng, Caird;
Twin screw; 9,000 IHP; 14, max
15 kn; Passengers: 1,100 3rd class.

1912 Oct 27: Launched.
1913 Mar: Completed.
London–Sydney service.
1914 Troop transport.
1919 Australia service again.
1930 May: Sold for breaking-up in
Japan.

1 *The* Ballarat *with the Blue Anchor Line funnel markings. Wm. Lund had to sell his Blue Anchor Line to P & O in 1910. P & O continued the service under the name of P & O Branch Line, and until 1914 allowed the ships to sail in the Blue Anchor Line colours.*
2 *The* Beltana, *second of the five B-class ships, entered service in 1912.*
3 *The* Benalla, *completed in 1913.*

Steamship *Berrima*
P & O Line, Greenock

Builders: Caird, Greenock
Yard no: 325
11,137 GRT; 157.0 × 19.0 m /
515 × 62.8 ft; IV exp eng, Caird;
Twin screw; 9,000 IHP; 14, max
15 kn; Passengers: 1,100 3rd class.

1913 Apr 15: Launched.
Dec: Completed. London–
Sydney service.
1914 Troop transport.
1920 Mar 24: First postwar
voyage London–Brisbane; then
again to Sydney.
1930 May: Sold for breaking-up in
Japan.

Steamship *Borda*
P & O Line, Greenock

Builders: Caird, Greenock
Yard no: 326
11,136 GRT; 157.0 × 19.0 m /
515 × 62.8 ft; IV exp eng, Caird;
Twin screw; 9,000 IHP; 14, max
15 kn; Passengers: 1,100 3rd class.

1913 Dec 17: Launched.
1914 Mar: Completed.
London–Sydney service.
Aug: Troop transport.
1920 London–Sydney again.
1928 Laid up.
1930 May: Sold for breaking-up in
Japan.

4

6

4/5 *The* Berrima *(4) as a troop transport during the First World War (5).*
6 *P & O Branch liner* Borda *leaving Cape Town.*

Kaiser Franz Josef I

Steamship *Kaiser Franz Josef I*
Unione Austriaca, Trieste

1919 *General Diaz*;
1920 *Presidente Wilson*;
1929 *Gange*; 1936 *Marco Polo*

Builders: Cant Nav Triestino,
Monfalcone
Yard no: 20
12,567 GRT; 152.4 × 18.9 m /
500 × 60.2 ft; IV exp eng, Rowan,
Glasgow; Twin screw; 13,000
IHP; 17, max 19 kn; Passengers:
160 1st class, 480 2nd class, 1,400
3rd class.

1911 Sep 11: Launched.
1912 Feb: Completed. Maiden
voyage Trieste–Buenos Aires.
May 9: First voyage Trieste–New
York.
1914 Aug: Laid up for duration of
war in Trieste.
1919 After Trieste had been given
up to Italy at the end of the First
World War, the Unione Austriaca
was re-founded and registered as
an Italian company under the
name Cosulich Societa Triestina
di Navigazione. The *Kaiser Franz
Josef I* was renamed *General
Diaz*.
1920 Renamed *Presidente
Wilson*, New York–Trieste
service.
1926 Converted to oil-firing at
Monfalcone. Passengers: 600
cabin and 3rd class.
1929 Sold to Lloyd Triestino.
Renamed *Gange*. Trieste–Far
East. Passengers: 236 1st class,
80 2nd class, 108 3rd class. 12,272
GRT.
1936 Refitted and modernised for
Venice–Alexandria service.
Passengers: 184 1st class, 58 2nd
class, 132 tourist class. Renamed
Marco Polo.
1937 Consequent upon
Government re-structuring of the
Italian merchant fleet, the *Marco
Polo* was transferred to
'Adriatica' SAN, Trieste.
1943 Following the Italian
capitulation, the ship was taken
over by the German firm,
Mediterranean Reederei GmbH.
1944 May 12: Sunk by the
Germans as a block-ship in the
harbour of La Spezia.
1949/50 Raised and broken up.

4

1 Kaiser Franz Josef I, *the flagship of the Unione Austriaca and the biggest passenger ship ever to sail under the Austrian flag.*
2 *After the First World War, the former* Kaiser Franz Josef I *sailed as the* Presidente Wilson *under the Italian flag; she then had shortened funnels.*
3 *The former* Kaiser Franz Josef I *after reconstruction as the* Gange *for Lloyd Triestino's Far East service.*
4 *After 25 years of service the ship was again thoroughly rebuilt and sailed as the* Marco Polo *between Venice and Alexandria.*

The D-Class of Royal Mail Lines

Steamship *Deseado*
Royal Mail Lines, Belfast

Builders: Harland & Wolff,
Belfast
Yard no: 420
11,477 GRT; 157.5 × 19.0 m /
517 × 62.3 ft; IV exp eng, H & W;
Twin screw; 8,000 IHP; 13.5, max
14.5 kn; Passengers: 95 1st class,
40 2nd class, 860 3rd class.

1911 Oct 26: Launched.
1912 Jun 27: Completed.
Jul 5: Maiden voyage
Liverpool–La Plata ports.
1934 Jul: Sold for breaking-up in
Japan.

Steamship *Demerara*
Royal Mail Lines, Belfast

Builders: Harland & Wolff,
Belfast
Yard no: 425
11,484 GRT; 157.5 × 19.0 m /
517 × 62.3 ft; IV exp eng, H & W;
Twin screw; 8,000 IHP; 13.5, max
14.5 kn; Passengers: 95 1st class,
38 2nd class, 860 3rd class.

1911 Dec 21: Launched.
1912 Aug 8: Completed.
Liverpool–La Plata service.
1933 Sold for breaking-up in
Japan.

Steamship *Desna*
Royal Mail Lines, Belfast

Builders: Harland & Wolff,
Belfast
Yard no: 426
11,484 GRT; 157.5 × 19.0 m /
517 × 62.3 ft; IV exp eng, H & W;
Twin screw; 8,000 IHP; 13.5, max
14.5 kn; Passengers: 95 1st class,
40 2nd class, 860 3rd class.

1912 Mar 2: Launched.
Jul: Completed. Liverpool–La
Plata service.
1933 Apr: Sold to shipbreakers in
Japan.

3

1

1 *The* Deseado, *which entered service in 1912, was the prototype of the five ships of the D-class.*
2 *Royal Mail liner* Demerara. *Because of their large refrigerated capacity the D-class ships remained in the La Plata service during the war.*
3 *The* Desna.

2

Steamship *Darro*
Royal Mail Lines, Belfast

Builders: Harland & Wolff,
Belfast
Yard no: 427
11,484 GRT; 157.5 × 19.0 m /
517 × 62.3 ft; IV exp eng, H & W;
Twin screw; 8,000 IHP; 13.5, max
14.5 kn; Passengers: 90 1st class,
40 2nd class, 860 3rd class.

1912 May 15: Launched.
Oct: Completed. Liverpool–La
Plata service. Actually built for
the Imperial Direct Line Ltd, a
company in the Elder Dempster
Group, the ship was at the outset
owned 100 per cent by Royal Mail
Lines. However, it was only later
in her career that she was
registered under Royal Mail
ownership.
1933 Apr: Sold for breaking-up in
Japan.

Steamship *Drina*
Royal Mail Lines, Belfast

Builders: Harland & Wolff,
Belfast
Yard no: 428
11,483 GRT; 157.5 × 19.0 m /
517 × 62.3 ft; IV exp eng, H & W;
Twin screw; 8,000 IHP; 13.5, max
14.5 kn; Passengers: 95 1st class,
40 2nd class, 860 3rd class.

1912 Jun 29: Launched.
1913 Jan: Completed.
Liverpool–La Plata service.
Originally registered for
Elder Line Ltd (Elder Dempster
Group), although owned 100 per
cent by Royal Mail.
1914 Hospital ship.
1915 Back in Liverpool–La Plata
service.

1917 Mar 1: The *Drina* was
torpedoed and sunk two nautical
miles west of the island of
Skokholm (Pembrokeshire coast)
by the German submarine UC 65.
15 dead.

4/5 Darro *and* Drina, *the last units of
the quintet.*

Steamship *Niagara*
Union SS Co of New Zealand,
London

Builders: Brown, Clydebank
Yard no: 415
13,415 GRT; 165.5 × 20.2 m /
543 × 66.3 ft; III exp eng plus
low pressure turbine; Triple screw;
14,500 IHP; 17, max 18 kn;
Passengers: 290 1st class, 223 2nd
class, 191 3rd class; Crew: 205.

1912 Aug 17: Launched.
1913 Mar: Completed.
Mar 12: Delivery voyage, Clyde
to Sydney.
May 5: Maiden voyage
Sydney–Vancouver.
1932 To Canadian Australasian
Line, London, a company formed
by Canadian Pacific and Union SS
Co to meet growing American and
Japanese competition on the
Pacific.
1940 Jun 19: On a voyage
Auckland–Vancouver, off Bream
Head, Whangarei, she ran into one
of the minefields laid by the
German auxiliary cruiser *Orion*.
The *Niagara* struck a mine and
sank in position 35°53′ S – 174°54′
E. Passengers and crew were able
to take to the boats and were
picked up by the British coaster
Kapiti and the Huddart Parker
liner *Wanganella*. Ten tons of gold
from the *Niagara's* cargo were
salvaged by divers from a depth of
nearly 500 feet in a remarkable
operation which took until the end
of 1941.

1 *The* Niagara *which sank after
hitting a mine in 1940.*

1

Turbine steamer *Empress of Russia*
Canadian Pacific, London

Builders: Fairfield, Glasgow
Yard no: 484
16,810 GRT; 180.4 × 20.8 m /
592 × 68.2 ft; Turbines, Fairfield;
Quadruple screw; 27,000 SHP; 20,
max 21.2 kn; Passengers: 284 1st
class, 100 2nd class, 808 Asiatic
steerage; Crew: 475.

1912 Aug 28: Launched.
1913 Mar 22: Delivered.
Apr 1: Maiden voyage
Liverpool–Hong Kong; then in
the line's Vancouver–Yokohama
service.
1914 Aug 23: Auxiliary cruiser.
1916 Feb 12: Transpacific service
again.
1918 May 6: Troop transport.
1919 Mar 8: Back to Canadian
Pacific after overhaul in Hong
Kong. Passengers: 350 1st class,
70 2nd class, 90 3rd class, 728
steerage.
1940 Nov 28: Troop transport.
1945 Sep 8: The *Empress of
Russia* caught fire in Barrow while
undergoing repairs and fitting-out
work and was totally destroyed.
1946 Broken up in Barrow by T.
W. Ward.

Turbine steamer *Empress of Asia*
Canadian Pacific, London

Builders: Fairfield, Glasgow
Yard no: 485
16,909 GRT; 180.4 × 20.8 m /
592 × 68.2 ft; Turbines, Fairfield;
Quadruple screw; 27,000 SHP; 20,
max 21.4 kn; Passengers: 284 1st
class, 100 2nd class, 808 Asiatic
steerage; Crew: 475.

1912 Nov 23: Launched.
1913 May: Completed.
Jun 14: Maiden voyage
Liverpool–Hong Kong; then
Vancouver–Yokohama service.
1914 Aug 2: Auxiliary cruiser.
1916 Mar 20: Transpacific service
again.
1918 May 3: Troop transport.
1919 Feb 10: Back to Canadian
Pacific after overhaul.
Passengers: 350 1st class, 70 2nd
class, 90 3rd class, 728 steerage.
Black hull 1919-26.
1926 Jan 11: The *Empress of Asia*
collided off Shanghai with the
British steamer *Tung Shing,* which
sank.
1941 Feb: Troop transport.
1942 Feb 5: With 2,651 people on
board the *Empress of Asia* was
attacked off Singapore for an hour
and a half by 27 Japanese aircraft.
After five direct bomb-hits, the
ship caught fire and sank nine
nautical miles from Keppel
Harbour. 19 dead.
1952. The International Salvage
Association began the scrapping
of the wreck.

1

2

3

1 *The* Empress of Russia, *the first large passenger ship to have a cruiser stern.*
2 *The* Empress of Russia *as a troop transport during the First World War.*
3/4 *Canadian Pacific liner* Empress of Asia. *For years the two sister-ships were the fastest liners on the Pacific.*

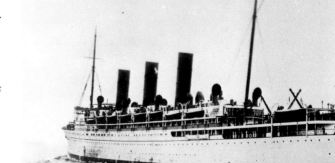

4

Steamship *Reina Victoria Eugenia*
Cia Trasatlantica, Barcelona

1931 *Argentina*

Builders: Swan, Hunter &
Wigham Richardson, Newcastle
Yard no: 884
10,137 GRT; 152.4 × 18.7 m /
500 × 61.3 ft; III exp eng plus
low pressure turbines from hull
builders; Quadruple screw;
10,840 IHP; 17, max 18.5 kn;
Passengers: 250 1st class, 100 2nd
class, 80 3rd class, 1,713 steerage.

1912 Sep 26: Launched.
1913 Feb 7: Trials.
Feb 16: Delivered. Used on
Spain–Cuba–Mexico route;
occasionally also to New York.
1931 Renamed *Argentina*. Used
mainly on Spain–South America
route.
1936 Mostly laid up after
outbreak of Spanish Civil War.
1939 Jan: Sunk in Barcelona by
Spanish Nationalist (Franco) air
attack.
Sep 8: Raised and laid up again.
1945 Sold for breaking-up.

Steamship *Infanta Isabel de
Borbon*
Cia Trasatlantica, Barcelona

1931 *Uruguay*

Builders: Denny, Dumbarton
Yard no: 969
10,348 GRT; 152.4 × 18.7 m /
500 × 61.3 ft; III exp eng plus
low pressure turbine; Triple
screw; 10,800 IHP; 17, max 18.6
kn; Passengers: 250 1st class, 100
2nd class, 75 3rd class, 1,700
steerage.

1912 Sep 28: Launched.
1913 Mar: Completed. Spain–
Cuba–Mexico service,
occasionally also New York
service.
1931 Renamed *Uruguay*. Used
mainly on Spain–South America
service.
1936 Mostly laid up after
outbreak of Spanish Civil War.
1939 Jan: Sunk in Barcelona by
Nationalist (Franco) air attack.
Jul 25: Raised.
1940 Broken up in Spain.

1 *The* Reina Victoria Eugenia *on trials.*
2 *The* Reina Victoria Eugenia *with a glassed-in bridge front and First World War neutrality markings in the form of the Spanish flag painted on her sides.*
3 *Like her sister-ship, the* Infanta Isabel de Borbon *also was a victim of the Spanish Civil War.*

1

2

3

Steamship *Kristianiafjord*
Norwegian America Line,
Christiania

Builders: Cammell, Laird & Co,
Birkenhead
Yard no: 784
10,669 GRT; 161.5 × 18.5 m /
530 × 61.2 ft; IV exp eng from hull
builders; Twin screw; 8,500 IHP;
15, max 17 kn; Passengers: 105 1st
class, 216 2nd class, 700 3rd class.

1912 Nov 23: Launched.
1913 May: Completed.
Jun 4: Maiden voyage Oslo
(Christiania)–New York.
1917 Jul 15: The *Kristianiafjord*
ran aground near Mistaken Point,
seven nautical miles from Cape
Race, and had to be abandoned as
a total loss.

1 *The* Kristianiafjord, *which was lost when she ran aground during the First World War.*

Steamship *Bergensfjord*
Norwegian America Line, Bergen

1946 *Argentina*; 1953 *Jerusalem*;
1957 *Aliya*

Builders: Cammell, Laird & Co,
Birkenhead
Yard no: 787
10,666 GRT; 161.5 × 18.5 m /
530 × 61.2 ft; IV exp eng from hull
builders; Twin screw; 8,500 IHP;
15, max 17 kn; Passengers: 105 1st
class, 216 2nd class, 760 3rd class.

1913 Apr 8: Launched.
Sep: Completed.
Sep 27: Maiden voyage Christiania
(Oslo)–New York.
1920 Converted to oil-firing.
1931 Refitted by AG 'Weser' in
Bremen. Low pressure turbine
added which raised her speed by
one knot. Passengers: 367 cabin
class, 572 3rd class; 11,015 GRT.
1938 Passengers: 90 cabin class,
155 tourist class, 500 3rd class.
1940 Apr: Laid up in New York.
Dec: Troop Transport under
British control but with

Norwegian crew. Managed by
Furness, Withy & Co.
1946 Feb: Back to Norwegian
America Line.
Nov: Sold to Home Lines,
Panama. Renamed *Argentina*.
Passengers: 32 1st class, 969
tourist class.
1947 Jan 13: First voyage
Genoa–La Plata.
1949 Sep: Genoa–Central
America service.
1952 Early part of year: First
voyage Genoa–New York.
1953 Feb: Sold to Zim Israel
Line, Haifa. Renamed *Jerusalem*.
Passengers: 33 1st class, 741
tourist class.
Apr 29: First voyage Haifa–New
York.
1955 Haifa–Marseille service.
1957 Renamed *Aliya*.
1958 May: Laid up.
1959 Aug 13: Arrived at La
Spezia. Broken up by Terrestre
Marittima.

2 *Norwegian America liner*
Bergensfjord *after refitting in 1931.*

3

4

3 *The* Bergensfjord *as troop transport during the Second World War.*
4/5 *Home Lines placed the former* Bergensfjord *into service in 1947 as the* Argentina. *When 40 years old, the ship changed hands yet again to become the* Jerusalem *(5), flagship of Zim Israel Line.*

5

White Star Liner Ceramic

Steamship *Ceramic*
White Star Line, Liverpool

Builders: Harland & Wolff, Belfast
Yard no: 432
18,481 GRT; 207.0 × 21.1 m / 679 × 69.4 ft; III exp eng plus low pressure turbine, H & W; Triple screw; 9,000 IHP; 15, max 16 kn; Passengers: 600 3rd class.

1912 Dec 11: Launched.
1913 Jul 5: Delivered.
Jul 24: Maiden voyage Liverpool–Sydney.
1914 Aug: Troop transport; from 1917 mainly cargo service on the Australian route.
1920 Nov 18: First postwar voyage Liverpool–Sydney.

1934 To Shaw, Savill & Albion, Southampton.
Aug 25: First voyage Liverpool–Brisbane.
1936 Reconstructed by Harland & Wolff at Govan. 18,713 GRT; Passengers: 480 cabin class. Reduced to 340 in 1938.
1940 Feb: Troop transport.
1942 Nov 23: The *Ceramic* left Liverpool for Australia for the last time. 656 people were on board.
Dec 7: The *Ceramic* was west of the Azores in position 40°30′ N – 10°20′ W when she was torpedoed by the German submarine U 515 within the first few minutes of the day. The explosion was so devastating that no radio call could be sent out. Only one man

survived the sinking of the *Ceramic;* he was taken aboard the U-boat. Not until much later did the British Admiralty discover where and when the *Ceramic* had sunk. The date of sinking given in British reports was December 6. This was based on British time by which the sinking actually took place at six minutes before midnight.

1 *The* Ceramic, *for years the largest ship sailing between Europe and Australia.*
2 *The* Ceramic *after reconstruction in 1936.*

Periodicals
Germanischer Lloyd, Register
(Berlin, Hamburg) from 1899
Lloyd's Register of Shipping
(London) from 1888
Weyer's Taschenbuch der
Kriegsflotten (Munich) from 1905

Magazines
Die Seekiste (Kiel) 1950–1964
Engineering (London) 1888–1920
Fairplay (London) 1913–1919
International Marine Engineering
(New York) 1899–1930
Marine News (Kendal) 1950–1972
Motorship (New York) 1921–1932
Schiffbau (Berlin) 1900–1939
Sea Breezes (Liverpool) 1949–1972
Shipbuilding and Shipping Record
(London) 1918–1930
The Belgian Shiplover (Brussels)
1959–1972
The Marine Engineer (London)
1890–1914
The Shipbuilder (London and
Newcastle) 1906–1937
Zeitschrift des Vereins deutscher
Ingenieure (Berlin) 1895–1914

Books
Anderson, *White Star* (Prescot) 1964
Bonsor, *North Atlantic Seaway*
(Prescot) 1955
Dunn, *Famous Liners of the Past,
Belfast Built* (London) 1964
Farquhar, *Union Fleet 1875–1968*
(Dunedin) 1968
Gröner, *Die deutschen Kriegsschiffe
1815–1945* (Munich) 1966
Hümmelchen, *Handelsstörer*
(Munich) 1967
Isherwood, *Steamers of the Past*
(Liverpool)
Kludas, *Die grossen deutschen
Passagierschiffe* (Oldenburg and
Hamburg) 1971
Le Fleming, *Blue Funnel Line*
(Southampton) 1961
Maber, *North Star to Southern Cross*
(Prescot) 1967
Michelsen, *Der U-Boots-Krieg
1914–1918* (Leipzig) 1925
Musk, *Canadian Pacific* (London)
1968

Overzier, *Der Amerikanisch-
Englische Schiffahrtstrust* (Berlin)
1912
Rohwer, *Die U-Boot-Erfolge der
Achsenmächte 1939–1945* (Munich)
1968

Other Sources
Archives and publications of
shipyards and shipping lines;
statements and reports in
newspapers.

I should like to register my very
sincere thanks for the kind loan of
photographs. The pictures in this
book were obtained from the
following sources:

Marius Bar, Toulon, pages 149/2,
157/3, 190/3
Dr H. Bischoff, Reinfeld, pages 33/1,
49/1, 51/3, 52/5, 145/5
Blohm+Voss AG, Hamburg, page
193/1
Canadian Pacific Steamships Ltd,
London, pages 69/7, 121/5, 126/3,
143/2, 203/1, 205/1 & 4
Compagnie Générale
Transatlantique, Paris, pages 76/1,
77/2 & 4, 147/1 & 2, 149/1
Cunard Steam-Ship Co Ltd, London,
pages 14/2, 79/1 & 3, 151/3, 181/3
Det Forenede Dampskibs-Selskab
A/S, Copenhagen, pages 94/1, 95/3 &
4
A. Duncan, Gravesend, pages 15/3,
29/14, 37/2, 39/5 & 6, 47/12, 66/3,
69/5, 71/8, 84/4, 97/2, 124/3, 133/6,
137/6, 151/2 & 4, 167/1, 173/1 & 2,
185/9, 187/3, 197/6, 199/2, 202/4,
205/3, 211/3, 213/1
Laurence Dunn, Richmond, page
53/6
Ian Farquhar, Dunedin, pages 151/1,
159/6
Hans Graf, Hamburg, pages 42/5,
49/2, 53/8, 63/3, 64/4, 73/1 & 2, 75/1 &
2, 91/1, 93/6, 97/5, 100/8, 101/1, 115/4,
117/6, 129/2, 153/2, 169/2, 171/4 & 5,
177/5, 191/1, 201/1 & 2

Hapag-Lloyd AG, Hamburg and
Bremen, pages 23/6, 25/10, 31/17 &
18, 33/3, 34/6, 51/4, 56/4, 57/5 & 6,
58/7, 59/9, 111/3, 121/4, 123/7 & 8,
143/1
Hans Hartz, Hamburg, page 111/4
E. K. Haviland, Baltimore, pages
71/9, 117/8, 163/5, 187/2, 195/1, 201/2
World Ship Photo Library, page 113/1
Imperial War Museum, London,
pages 11/1, 17/1, 39/1, 77/3
R. J. Innes, Halifax, page 211/5
A. Lagendijk, Enschede, page 65/6
M. Lindenborn, Capelle a. d. IJssel,
page 65/5
Mariners Museum, Newport News,
page 13/3
H. J. Mayburg, Bremen, pages 18/1,
19/3, 87/3, 113/2, 140/4, 141/1-3, 207/2
Dr J. Meyer, Rellingen, pages 143/4,
145/6
Norske Amerikalinje A/S, Oslo,
pages 209/1, 210/2
Peninsular and Oriental Steam
Navigation Co, London, pages 103/1
& 2, 105/3 & 4, 107/6 & 8, 159/5 & 7,
195/2
Provincial Archives, Victoria, BC,
page 205/2
Real Photographs, Broadstairs, page
193/2
Royal Mail Lines Ltd (Furness Withy
Group), London, pages 129/1, 131/5,
133/7 & 8
Steamship Historical Society of
America, pages 27/13, 88/5
All other photographs are from the
author's collection.